FREUD AND HIS MOTHER

FREUD AND HIS MOTHER

Preoedipal Aspects of Freud's Personality

Deborah P. Margolis

JASON ARONSON INC.
Northvale, New Jersey
London

This book was set in 11 point Bem by TechType of Upper Saddle River, New Jersey, and printed and bound by Book-mart Press of North Bergen, New Jersey.

10 9 8 7 6 5 4 3 2 1

Library of Congress Cataloging-in-Publication Data

Margolis, Deborah P.
Freud and his mother: preoedipal aspects of Freud's personality / by Deborah P. Margolis.
p. cm.
Includes bibliographical references (p.) and index.
ISBN 1-56821-448-0
1. Freud, Sigmund, 1856–1939. 2. Psychoanalysts—Austria—Biography. 3. Freud, Amalia, 1835–1929. 4. Mothers and sons. 5. Oedipus complex. I. Title.
BF109.F74M36 1995
150.19′52′092—dc20
[B] 94-44328

Manufactured in the United States of America. Jason Aronson Inc. offers books and cassettes. For information and catalog write to Jason Aronson Inc., 230 Livingston Street, Northvale, New Jersey 07647.

For Benjamin David,

Helen, Melvin, Daniel, and Emily

Contents

Preface

"... there is no man so great," Freud wrote in his study of Leonardo da Vinci, "as to be disgraced by being subject to the laws which govern both normal and pathological activity with equal cogency." But Freud, it seems, in his need for privacy, was averse to having this dictum applied to himself, strenuously objecting to being made the subject of biography. His need for privacy, however, has not prevailed, for no man as great as he or as Leonardo can avoid being made the subject of biographical study.

Drawing on the study of his own unconscious and on that of his patients, Freud discovered the Oedipus complex, a complex distasteful to the world at large though long intuitively known to men of genius in the literary field. Yet master though he was at unraveling the conflicts of the Oedipus complex, Freud did not continue to the preoedipal period of life, perhaps constrained by a reluctance to deal with the complexes of his own earliest years. It is as though he had resolved: to this point and no further. And who knows but that there was deep wisdom is this resolve, if such it was. In a letter to his friend and colleague, Sandor Ferenczi, Freud wrote: "A man should not strive to eliminate his complexes but to get into accord with them: they are legitimately what directs his conduct in the world."

There can be no doubt that Freud's complexes not only directed his conduct in the world, but were also major factors in directing his creativity. "Our complexes," he remarked to an interviewer, "are the sources of our weakness; they are also often the source of our strength." Freud was content to live with his weakness, leaving unexplored and unresolved the complexes which were also the source of his strength. But the limits he set for himself he could not impose on others, so great is the urge to penetrate to the sources of greatness. And so—albeit without his nod of approval—the literature on Freud continues to proliferate, a tribute to the man who, ironically, developed the tools used to reach the deeper layers of the human psyche which he was reluctant to explore. This work is a study of Freud's preoedipal complexes which have so richly endowed our civilization.

Acknowledgments

Unlike Athena, who sprang full blown from the brow of Zeus, a book is beholden for its conception and birth to many influences, some tangible, some less clearly defined, though equally potent. For a number of years Theodor Reik was a frequent guest at our dinner table. "Freud climbed the stairs to my attic room to give me the prize . . . ," "Freud said to me . . . ," "Freud told me that . . . ," "Once, when I took a walk with Freud . . . ," "Martha followed us out of the house and said, 'Sigmund, you forgot your galoshes.' " These were constants of the memorable hours he spent at our dinner table. Was it our love of Reik and his love of his old master that first pointed the way?

I am no less indebted to Hyman Spotnitz, who expanded my psychoanalytical horizons and guided my entrance into the field. My daughter Helen's very existence was a spur to productivity. I wish, further, to express my gratitude to Marie Coleman Nelson for reading the manuscript in its first draft and encouraging me to carry on, to Lawrence Epstein, for his heartening enthusiasm, to Phyllis and Cyril Meadow, for providing the professional setting conducive to analytic research and for their moral support, to Evelyn and Leonard Liegner, for their nurturing friendship.

I am also most grateful to Michael Moskowitz and Judy Cohen of Jason Aronson, to Michael for his prompt and hearty endorsement of the manuscript and to Judy for performing with skill and aplomb the numerous tasks that go into turning a manuscript into a book.

My indebtedness to my husband, Benjamin David, is incalculable. I am grateful to him for his erudition, his clarifying perceptions and insights, his personal involvement, his sustaining love and support. Without him this book, literally, would not have been written.

1

I AM THE MOTHER

> I have found that people who know they are preferred by their mother give evidence in their lives of a peculiar self-reliance and an unshakable optimism which often seem like heroic attributes and bring actual success to their possessors.
>
> —Freud

Freud was born in a caul. This unusual circumstance was a source of delight to his mother, Amalia, for according to folklore a child so born was destined to a life of happiness and fame. In quick succession seven additional children were born (the second, Julius, died in infancy). Of her seven surviving children, Sigmund, her first-born, remained Amalia's favorite, *mein goldener Sigi, Sigi, mein Gold.* Amalia's belief that Sigmund was destined to greatness was reinforced by the prophecy of an old peasant woman she met in a pastry shop. "It became one of the constantly repeated family stories, a part of the atmosphere in which the child grew up. Thus the hero's garb was in the weaving, right at the cradle" (Bernfeld and Bernfeld 1944,

p. 189). "Could this," Freud asks himself, "have been the source of my thirst for grandeur?" (1900, 4:192). Could Freud, master solver of riddles, have seriously asked this question? Perhaps it was his sister Anna who more accurately identified the source of her brother's thirst for grandeur. "My mother," writes Anna Freud Bernays (1940), "hoped great things for her first-born, and treasured early incidents which gave body to her hopes. Perhaps my mother's trust in Sigmund's future destiny played a definite part in the trend given his whole life" (pp. 140–141). Amalia's trust in her son's destiny, it seems, not only gave impetus to his striving, but also resonated in his psychological conceptualizations. Thus, theorizing about Goethe, he theorized about himself:

> . . . if a man has been his mother's undisputed darling he retains throughout life the triumphant feeling, the confidence in success, which not seldom brings actual success along with it. And Goethe might well have given some such heading to his autobiography as: "My strength has its roots in my relation to my mother" [1917, 17:156]

Amalia was twenty-one years old when Sigmund was born and her husband, Jakob, forty-one. At the time of Sigmund's birth the Freuds occupied one of the two rooms over a locksmith shop in the town of Freiberg, in Moravia, the second room being occupied by the owner and his family. An impecunious wool merchant, Jakob, hoping for better fortune elsewhere, removed his family—then consisting of Amalia, Sigmund, aged three, and Anna—from Freiberg, and after a year in Leipzig, came to Vienna and settled in Leopoldstadt, the Jewish quarter of the city. But here, too, fortune evaded him. Gentle, mild-mannered, kindly, "always hopefully expecting something to turn up," as Freud described him in a letter to his future wife, Martha Bernays, Jakob was often obliged to receive help from his or his wife's relatives, among them the two sons of a former marriage who had emigrated to England and established themselves there as businessmen.

Unschooled in, or perhaps indifferent to, the material ways of the world, Jakob was yet held in high esteem by his children. On Jakob's death at the age of eighty-one Freud (1985a) wrote to his friend Fliess: "I valued him highly, understood him very well, and with his peculiar mixture of deep wisdom and fantastic light-heartedness he had a significant effect on my life" (p. 202). Nor were his grandchildren lacking in affection for their grandfather. Martin, Freud's eldest son, who was seven years old when Jakob died, recalled him as being loved and respected by all and "terribly nice with us children. He brought us small presents and he used to tell us stories, mostly with a little twinkle in his great brown eyes, as if he wanted to say, 'Isn't everything we are doing and saying here a great joke?' " (M. Freud 1958, p. 10).

And what were Martin's reflections on his grandmother Amalia?

> Grandmother came from East Galicia . . . and it might not be known by many people that Galician Jews were a peculiar race, not only different from any other races inhabiting Europe, but absolutely different from Jews who had lived in the West for some generations. They, these Galicians, had little grace and no manners, and their women were certainly not what we should call "ladies." They were highly emotional and easily carried away by their feelings. But, although in many respects they would seem to be untamed barbarians to more civilized people, they, alone of all minorities, stood up against the Nazis. It was men of Amalia's race who fought the German army on the ruins of Warsaw. . . .
>
> These people are not easy to live with, and grandmother, a true representative of her race, was no exception. She had great vitality and much impatience; she had a hunger for life and an indomitable spirit. Nobody envied Aunt Dolfi, whose destiny it was to dedicate her life to the care of an old mother who was a tornado. Aunt Dolfi once took Amalia to buy a new hat—and she was not perhaps

> wise to recommend what seemed to her "something suitable." Studying carefully her image crowned by the hat she had agreed to try on, Amalia, who was on the wrong side of ninety, finally shouted, "I won't take this one; it makes me look old" [M. Freud 1958, p. 11]

Judith Bernays Heller, daughter of Anna Freud who married Eli Bernays (the brother of Freud's wife Martha), lived with her maternal grandparents during the year when her parents were in America, where they had gone to establish a home. Judith reflected in later years on her tornado of a grandmother and her kindly grandfather.

> I cannot say who really supported the establishment. I do know that my grandfather was no longer working, but divided his time between reading the Talmud (in the original) at home, sitting in a coffee house, and walking in the park. Occasionally, he took me with him, when the others were too busy to occupy themselves with me. Tall and broad, with a long beard, he was very kind and gentle, and humorous in the bargain—much more so than my grandmother, who [*sic*] I really feared, though I admired her stateliness and the nice clothes she wore when she went out with her friends. . . . My grandmother . . . who had a volatile temperament, would scold the maid as well as her daughters and rushed about the house. . . . There was no mistaking her lack of interest in all that concerned me. . . . She was very charming when strangers were about, but I at least, always felt that with familiars she was a tyrant, and a selfish one (1956, pp. 335–338).

For many years Amalia spent her summers at Ischl, a summer resort, and for as many years her daughter Dolfi, designated by the family to look after her, followed in her wake. Amalia spent her afternoons playing cards with her friends and acquaintances at the tea and coffee "stations" in the woods and villages around Ischl. "My aunt," writes Judith, "who did not play cards, would be forced to go with her, whether she liked it or not" (p. 336).

When Dolfi was in her early twenties Freud described her in a letter to Martha as "the sweetest and best of my sisters, has such a great capacity for deep feeling and alas an all-too-fine sensitiveness" (1960, p. 58). We learn of the fate of this sister after her many years of attendance on Amalia from another of Freud's letters, this letter written to Dolfi on her sixty-eighth birthday: "The enclosed is just some pocket money for your birthday for which I send you my best wishes as well as my most heartfelt gratitude for your invaluable services throughout all these years. As you know, we shall be in Mother's immediate neighborhood this summer, but unfortunately I don't yet know when" (1960, p. 397).

Freud wrote to his sixty-eight year old sister that he would be in Mother's immediate neighborhood. Was it not Dolfi's neighborhood as well? His gratitude, and no doubt the gratitude of all concerned, must have been heartfelt indeed for Dolfi's invaluable services of taking Amalia off their hands. ". . . it might be true to say," writes Martin, "that constant attendance on Amalia had suppressed her personality into a condition of dependence from which she never recovered" (M. Freud 1958, p. 16). More than suppressed, Dolfi's personality seems to have been so completely expunged that even her brother Sigmund, a man of extraordinary empathy and delicacy of feeling and in former days so finely attuned to his sister's sensitiveness, came to regard her as a mere appendage to their mother. Amalia died when she was ninety-five and Dolfi approaching the age of seventy. Long drained of whatever resources she might once have had, Amalia's death left her, Judith recalls, "completely broken and without any interest or purpose in life. Only later, when two of her widowed sisters came to live with her . . . did her spirits pick up again" (1956, p. 338).

And how fared Amalia's favorite with his mother? If the hero's garb was in the weaving right at the cradle, then it behooved him to please the weaver. Neither could the message implicit in *mein goldener Sigi* be easily misconstrued. From as far back as he could remember, the golden son, preferred above all others by his mother, realized that to remain preferred he must achieve. "Just suppose, darling girl," he wrote to Martha when he was twenty-six, "that success corresponded precisely to the merit of the individual, would not love tend to lose some of its purity? I would not be sure whether it were me you loved or the recognition given to me, and if misfortune befell me the girl could say: I do not love you any more, your unworthiness is proven" (1960, pp. 26–27). Where but from his experience with his mother could Freud have derived this grim view of a woman's love? He bluntly expresses his heart's desire in a dream: "I wish I might for once experience love that cost me nothing" (1900, 5:672).

"I believe that people see something alien in me," Freud wrote to Martha at the age of thirty, "and the real reason for this is that in my youth I was never young and now that I am entering the age of maturity I cannot mature properly" (1960 p. 202). Identified since his earliest days with his mother's hopes and aspirations for him and assuming the burden of her expectations, he felt himself alien to the carefree world of his childhood peers. Projectively, he then experienced the world as seeing "something alien" in him. In the same vein, years later, he wrote in a letter to Jung: ". . . I have always felt that there is something about my personality, my ideas and manner of speaking, that people find strange and repellent . . ." (Freud and Jung 1974, p. 82). How explain so deprecatory a self-evaluation from one who was his mother's favorite? Could Freud have sensed his repressed feelings of rage against his mother and found them "strange and repellent"? In another letter to Martha: "I consider it a great misfortune that nature has not granted me that indefinite something which attracts people. I believe it is this lack more than any other which has deprived me of a rosy existence" (1960, p. 199). We would perhaps be more in touch with Freud's unconscious in this instance if we were to substitute the word mother for nature.

Freud's feeling of alienation may well have been a determinant of his tendency to distance himself, of a preference for the ivory tower. The acclaim following on the heels of his growing fame seemed to him almost an irritant, "a popularity that I find repellent," an invasion of the privacy he had come to cherish. "Freud found his increasing popularity only a burden," writes Jones (1957, p. 83). And complaining to Jones of the consequences of the success he had in earlier years so ardently desired: "I have so much business correspondence to do, warning patients not to come as I have not the time to treat them and declining flattering offers to write a paper on such a subject for such a periodical. These are the drawbacks of popularity. I see not much of its blessings" (Jones 1957, p. 83). The sixth International Psychoanalytical Congress, with its attendance of sixty-two members and fifty-seven guests, proved an unexpected success, a cause, in the psychoanalytic community, for rejoicing. ". . . when the excitement had died down, Freud's feelings of satisfaction gave way to a more critical attitude towards the outer world" (Jones 1957, p. 28). And when his friend Pfister wrote to Freud, congratulating him on the progress of psychoanalysis, he responded:

> It is true that things are moving everywhere, but you seem to over-estimate my pleasure in that. What personal pleasure is to be derived from analysis I obtained during the time when I was alone, and since others have joined me it has given me more pain than pleasure. The way people accept and distort it has not changed the opinion I formed of them when they non-understandingly rejected it. An incurable breach must have come into existence at that time between me and other men. [Freud and Pfister 1963, p. 79]

It seems more likely that the incurable breach came into existence far earlier than Freud was aware of, at the time of his infancy, when his hero's garb was in the weaving. More comfortable in the shadows than in the limelight, he resented what he saw as the intrusion of others into a world he had created for himself the better to realize his mother's hopes and aspirations. Writing in *The History of the Psychoanalytic Movement* of that trying period when he was rejected by his peers, and forgetful perhaps of his moods of depression and despair, he recalled it as a period of idyllic existence: "Meanwhile, like Robinson Crusoe, I settled down as comfortably as possible on my desert island. When I look back to those lonely years, away from the pressures and confusions of today, it seems like a glorious heroic age. My 'splendid isolation' was not without its advantages and charm" (14:22). From his splendid isolation Freud had written to Fliess: "In the evening I would like something that cheers, refreshes, and clears things away, but I am always alone" (1985a, p. 398). Hindsight, apparently, did not always serve Freud well. What kept him from succumbing to his self-doubt in the face of the continued indifference of his peers may well have been Fliess's encouragement and the indomitable spirit of his introjected mother.

The bond between mother and son was never broken. ". . . there was throughout a close attachment between the two" (Jones 1953, p. 3). Just how close may be gathered from Martin's description of a family gathering held in his grandmother's house:

> . . . always, as the evening went on, an atmosphere of growing crisis was felt by all as Amalia became unsettled and anxious. There are people who, when they are unsettled and disturbed, will hide these feelings because they do not want to affect the peace of those around them; but Amalia was not one of these. My father always came to these gatherings—I know of no occasion when he disappointed her—but his working day was a long one and he always came much later than anyone else. Amalia knew this, but perhaps it was a reality she could never accept. Soon she would be seen running anxiously to the door and out to the

> landing to stare down the staircase. Was he coming? Where was he? Was it not getting very late? This running in and out might go on for an hour, but it was known that any attempt to stop her would produce an outburst of anger which it would be better to avoid by taking as little notice as possible. And my father always came at very much the usual time, but never at a moment when Amalia was waiting for him on the landing. [M. Freud 1958, p. 12]

A most instructive description of the quality of Amalia's love for her son. It was obviously compounded by a demand for instant gratification and rage at the inevitable frustration that such a demand produced. One wonders why, remarkably, Amalia was never on the landing to greet her son when he arrived.

Equally revealing of the nature of Amalia's love for her favorite was her participation in his seventieth birthday celebration. Wishing to spare her—an old woman of ninety-one—the trouble of coming to his house for the celebration which was to be held the following day, Freud came to his mother the evening before to receive her congratulations. But to no avail. The next day, the first guest to ring the bell at Berggasse 19 was Amalia. Her granddaughter Judith (Heller 1956) adds a few details to the story of Amalia's attendance at the celebration:

> When there was a special invitation, as for instance to the celebration of my Uncle Sigmund's seventieth birthday in 1926 . . . she insisted that she be bought a new dress and hat to go to the *Jause* (coffee party) at his house. She had to be carried down the stairs from her own home, and up the stairs to the Freuds, but she did not mind that so long as she could be present to be honored and feted as the mother of her "golden son," as she called her Sigmund. [p. 338]

That she had a just claim to her son's distinction Amalia established beyond cavil to at least one of Freud's students in her self-introduction: "I am the mother" (Roazen 1976, p. 46).

From the beginning, Amalia strove to remove whatever obstacles she felt might stand in the way of her son's march to greatness. And the son, feeling the way the wind blew, exerted his own tyranny in the service of the goal he shared with her. "In spite of his youth," writes his sister Anna,

> Sigmund's word and wish were respected by everyone in the family. When I was eight years old my mother, who was very musical, wanted me to study the piano, and I began practicing by the hour. Though Sigmund's room was not near the piano, the sound disturbed him. He appealed to my mother to remove the piano if she did not wish him to leave the house altogether. The piano disappeared and with it all opportunity for his sisters to become musicians. [Bernays 1940, p. 142]

Since it was the norm for girls of the middle class to study the piano, its disappearance was an egregious breach of the cultural values of the day. As for Amalia, being musical and desirous of a musical education for her daughters, it was the price she must pay for her favoritism. Significantly, it was not to the father but to the mother that the son addressed his appeal. There seems to have been no question of who ruled the roost.

When Freud was nineteen and a university student, the family moved to a flat with three bedrooms. The bedrooms were shared by parents, five sisters, and Alexander, the youngest of the brood and ten years Freud's junior. To Sigmund was assigned the "cabinet," a room facing the street. Here he slept, studied, entertained his friends, and on occasion took his meals. The bedrooms were lit by candles; Sigmund's room alone was furnished with an oil lamp. Thus mother and son in pursuit of a common goal.

"It was strange to a young visitor to hear her [Amalia] refer to the great Master as '*mein goldener Sigi*' " (Jones 1953, p. 3). And so she continued to call him to the end of her days, even when he was old and grey. Some of Freud's more intimate student-patients "made it a point," writes Judith (Heller 1956), "of paying their respects to her regularly" (p. 338). How explain this most unusual practice? Was it at the suggestion of their analyst? Or was it, perhaps, out of identification with their analyst's excessive attachment to his mother?

According to Jones (1953) Freud mentioned his mother in only two connections, "that she was very given to complaining, and that she suffered from a severe tuberculosis of the lung" (and from which she recovered) (pp. 157–158). A rare occasion when Freud broke his reticence about Amalia was a visit to the Binswangers. Binswanger (1957) writes that on this visit Freud spoke of his "great mother attachment" (p. 42). It would be instructive to know what Freud had to say about this attachment. Binswanger does not enlighten us, but we may conjecture, from a letter Freud wrote to Martha in 1884, when he was twenty-eight, the tenor of his communication. "My mother is a fragile woman both physically and spiritually, but I offer her the most sincere apologies in case I have not done justice to her. I do not know one action of hers in which she has followed her own moods or interests against the interests or happiness of one of her children" (1985b, p. 99).

This is idealization indeed. Martin and Judith, viewing Amalia years later with the unclouded eyes of childhood, saw quite a different Amalia. So, apparently, had Freud in earlier days. In 1872, when Freud was sixteen, he visited the Fluss family in Freiberg, old friends of the Freuds who had remained in the small Moravian town and prospered. One of the Fluss children was Gisela, a girl a year or two younger than Freud, to whom "I took a fancy," Freud reported in a letter to his friend Eduard Silberstein. In a subsequent letter to his friend he elaborated on the qualities of Gisela's mother:

> Would you believe that this woman from a middle-class background, who once lived in fairly straitened circumstances, has acquired an education of which a nineteen-

> year-old salon-bred young thing would not be ashamed? She has read a great deal, including the classics, and what she has not read she is conversant with. . . . She is even knowledgeable about politics, participates fully in the affairs of the little town, and, I think, it is she above all who is guiding the household into the modern mainstream. But don't therefore take her for a frustrated bluestocking. I have seen for myself that she plays as large a part in running the business as Herr Fluss. . . . And you should see how she has brought up and continues to bring up her seven children . . . how no concern of any of them ceases to be hers. . . . I have never seen *such* superiority before. Other mothers—and why disguise the fact that our own are among them? We shan't love them the less for it—care only for the physical well-being of their sons. . . . I have never seen her in a bad mood, or rather, vent her mood on the innocent. . . . [1990, p. 17]

Clearly, the sixteen-year-old Freud would have preferred a mother like Frau Fluss to his own. And as clearly, he hastened to deny his critical attitude with the reassurance that "We shan't love them the less for it." So well did repression do its work that years later he was able to write of Amalia to Martha in the most glowing terms.

Freud's idealization of his mother persisted throughout his life. On his seventy-fifth birthday the town of Freiberg celebrated the occasion by placing a bronze commemorative tablet on the house where he was born. Freud's daughter Anna attended the ceremony, bringing with her a letter from her father to the Burgomaster of the town: ". . . deeply buried within me there still lives the happy child of Freiberg, the first-born son of a youthful mother, who received his first indelible impressions from this air, from this soil" (Freud 1931b, 21:259).

Freud seems here to be carried away by the requirements of the ceremonial occasion. Forgotten are his complaints that he had been deprived of a rosy existence and that as a youth he was never young. There is no question that he received indelible impressions from the air and soil of Freiberg, but we may safely say that equally indelible were the impressions he received from a mother who believed firmly in his future greatness and, to reach that goal, placed upon him as early as his first three years of life the burden of her own frustrated ambition. A young man still in his twenties, Freud wrote to Martha: ". . . to have you completely is the one condition I make to life, which I otherwise don't set any great store by" (1960, p. 113). This bleak outlook seems hardly compatible with one who set out as the happy child of Freiberg. Freud describes himself as the son of a youthful mother. What has happened to Jakob, whom, as he had acknowledged to Fliess, he had valued highly and who had had a significant effect on his life? In an early letter to Martha, Freud described himself as the "duplicate of his father physically and to some extent mentally" as well (Jones 1953, p. 2). Seeing himself, to some extent, as a mental duplicate of his father, is highly suggestive. Jakob is reported by his granddaughter Judith as spending his time at home reading the Talmud in the original. This would indicate an uncommon degree of learning, particularly for a wool merchant, a man whose chief preoccupation was not rabbinical scholarship. On Sigmund's thirty-fifth birthday Jakob presented him with a treasured possession he had acquired as a young man which he rebound in leather for the presentation to his son, the Ludwig Philippson Bible in Hebrew and German. The lengthy inscription, written in Hebrew, indicates an intimate knowledge of the original Hebrew text. In his inscription, Jakob reminds his son that when he [Sigmund] was seven years old, the "Spirit of the Lord began to move you and said to you: Go, read My Book that I have written and there will be opened to you the sources of wisdom, of knowledge and understanding. See the Book of Books, from which the lawmakers learnt law and justice . . ." (Krüll 1986, p. 134). "My deep engrossment in the Bible story (almost as soon as I had learnt the art of reading)," Freud wrote, "had, as I recognized much later, an enduring effect upon the direction of my interest" (1925, 20:8). We may say that although Amalia may have been the driving force in her son's will to achieve greatness, his reverence for wisdom and understanding he imbibed from Jakob. And even those indelible impressions Freud claims to have received from the air and soil of Freiberg may well have been in large part Jakob's doing. As a toddler, Freud was taken by his father on walks through the fields and forests not far from his home. In a passage in *Screen Memories*, Freud speaks through a patient (a thinly disguised representative of himself) of his walks with his father: "I believe now that I was never free from a longing for the beautiful woods near our home, in which (as one of the memories from those days tells me) I used to run off from my father, almost before I had learnt to walk" (1899, 3:312–313). This would suggest that the toddler played the game of tag or hide-and-seek with his light-hearted father, and that in the happy hours of his rambles in the woods was rooted his deep and abiding love for the country and for scenic beauty. Yet in his letter to the Burgomaster Freud makes no mention of his father. Like his daughter Dolfi, Jakob appears to have been expunged.

Since there can be no quarrel with the proposition that early experiences help shape the man, and perhaps taking their cue from Freud himself, biographers of Freud have sought to give credit where they believe credit is due. An obvious candidate is Freud's mother. Hence Eissler (1985):

> Freud is one of the few great men whose relationships with women were happy. . . . Without a doubt he had a particularly harmonious relationship with his mother. She was not an extraordinary woman, but she must have had a very deep understanding of the child, because he was able to develop to the full under her care. [p. 29]

An encomium Amalia would have endorsed.

Amidst the general adulation of Freud's mother, Schur (1972) sounds a cautionary note: "In the same summer Freud's mother died at the age of 95. . . . Whatever Freud's early relationship to his mother had been, during her last years it was, at least outwardly, one of cordial filial duty. I had never met her, and Freud had spoken of her very little. There was no obvious grief upon her death . . ." (p. 423). Krüll (1986), less discreet, appraises Freud's mother: "In contrast to most of his biographers, I hold that Amalia was not a giving mother figure but one who loved her son demandingly and selfishly" (p. 118). Holt (1992) sees the intensity of Freud's driving ambition as due in part to his wish to please his demanding mother, "to an underlying sense that if he could once attain greatness, perhaps at last his mother would love him wholeheartedly, warmly, and for his own sake" (p. 8).

Freud's denial of hostile feelings toward his mother is implicit in an idealization of her which defied reality. If denial is to be maintained, one must develop a caution, a reserve, lest, with the lessening of control, the unwanted feelings in the unconscious slip from their moorings and rise to the surface. Freud was a man of reserve with a strong need for privacy. Jones (1955) reflects on this need:

> . . . there were features about his attitude that would seem to pass beyond that and to justify the word privacy being replaced by secrecy. For it would hold good when there were no particular reasons for the privacy or concealment; and then, again, its strength was really remarkable . . . somehow he managed to convey the impression that only what he vouchsafed about his personality was a permissible topic and that he would resent any intimate questioning. He never spoke to his children about his youth and early years; most of the knowledge they have of it has come from the present work (pp. 408–409).

Freud's concealment went beyond the characterological, extending, at times, to his physical bearing. Andreas-Salomé (1964) writes, after attending a lecture by Freud:

> Home with Tausk and Federn . . . Spoke about Freud. Tausk at such times speaks passionately. A lot of it fits my external picture of Freud, especially, for example, as he enters the class with the appearance of moving to the side. There is in this gesture a will to solitude, a concealment of himself within his own purposes, which by his preference would be no concern of his school or his public. [p. 46]

Freud's compulsion to conceal—a bane to his biographers—reached far back to days before he was assailed by the public clamor he came to abhor. As a young man of twenty-nine he informed Martha, on changing his living quarters, that he had destroyed all his papers, notes and manuscripts, letters—except those of his family ("Yours, my darling, were never in danger")—an action "yet unborn and unfortunate people will one day resent. . . . I am referring to my biographers. . . . I am already looking forward to seeing them go astray" (1960, pp. 140–141). Again, in 1907, he destroyed a mass of documents and letters, "greatly to our loss," Jones laments. And yet again, leaving Vienna when he was eighty-two for his final home in England, he destroyed papers and correspondence, his daughter Anna and Marie Bonaparte rescuing from his wastebasket what they could.

It seems that Jones, Freud's official biographer, who complained that what Freud revealed of his life was "far more carefully selected and censored than is generally supposed," was at times indeed led astray. Speculating on the motives for Freud's need for concealment, Jones (1955) writes: "One must suppose that in Freud's earliest years there had been extremely strong motives for concealing some important phase of his development—perhaps even from himself. I would venture to surmise it was his deep love for his mother" (p. 409). But why forever be secretive about this oedipal love, particularly since he had openly declared it in his *Interpretation of Dreams* and established its universality?

We would surmise, rather, that what Freud found it

necessary to conceal, even from himself—perhaps above all from himself—was not his love, but his repressed hate for his mother. How else explain the vehemence with which he thwarted every effort to penetrate to his early years? Invited in 1929 by an American publisher to write an autobiography, he responded: "That is of course quite an impossible suggestion. . . . A psychologically complete and honest confession of life . . . would require so much indiscretion . . . about family, friends, and enemies . . . that it is simply out of the question. What makes all autobiographies worthless is, after all, their mendacity . . ." (1960, p. 391). What is revealing in Freud's characterization of biography and autobiography is his use of the words confession and mendacity, confession being associated with sin or wrongdoing, and mendacity with concealment of the truth. For Freud a biography seemed to imply a confession of what one wished to conceal.

Even more vehement, when he was eighty, was his rejection of his friend Arnold Zweig's offer to write his biography:

> . . . only today . . . can I settle down and write you a letter, alarmed by the threat that you want to become my biographer—you, who have so much better and more important things to do, you who can establish monarchs and who can survey the brutal folly of mankind from a lofty vantage point; no, I am far too fond of you to permit such a thing. Anyone who writes a biography is committed to lies, concealments, hypocrisy, flattery and even to hiding his lack of understanding, for biographical truth does not exist, and if it did we could not use it.
>
> Truth is unobtainable, mankind does not deserve it, and in any case is not our Prince Hamlet right when he asks who would escape whipping were he used after his dessert? [Freud and Zweig 1970, p. 127]

Freud had quoted Hamlet's query twenty-nine years earlier when, in the midst of his self-analysis, he had disclosed to Fliess that he had discovered the Oedipus complex.

> A single idea of general value dawned on me. I have found, in my own case too, [the phenomenon of] being in love with my mother and jealous of my father, and I now consider it a universal event in early childhood. . . . How does he [Hamlet] explain his irresolution in avenging his father by murder of his uncle. . . . How better than through the torment he suffers from the obscure memory that he himself had contemplated the same deed against his father out of passion for his mother, and—"use every man after his dessert," and who should " 'scape whipping?" [1985a, pp. 272–273]

Since Freud had long ago dredged up his Oedipus complex from his unconscious and was no longer tormented by its obscure memory, why his objection to Zweig's writing his biography? Was he, perhaps, tormented by the still obscure memory of his hostility toward his mother, which, if brought to consciousness, would dictate that he not escape whipping? And since Freud, as he declared in a letter to Putnam (1960), considered himself to be a very moral human being, with a sense of justice and consideration for others, one who disliked making others suffer or taking advantage of them, who had not only never done anything mean or malicious but was never even tempted to do so, we must assume that his objection to a biography stemmed from a reason to which only his unconscious was privy.

Only rarely, as in a letter to Fliess, are we permitted a glimpse of what lay behind Freud's idealization of his mother. Eager to visit his friend in Berlin, Freud finds himself obliged to forego the pleasure of the visit. As one of the hindrances to his coming, he writes: "My own mother is there now as well, with my sister, and I would of necessity have to devote a part of my already short time to her" (1985a, p. 306). "Of necessity" would hardly rank as filial love. Also, the throw-away reference to his sister calls for a bit of exploration. Was the sister Dolfi? If so, his offhand mention of her is further indication of her lowly status. It is solely to his mother that he must devote a part of his time. Was the sister Marie, who lived in Berlin and whom perhaps Amalia was visiting? If so, neither did she merit a part of his time. Only the mother could command and receive. In another letter to Fliess, Freud (1985a) writes: "On the Thursday after our parting, I was forced by circumstances to take a four-hour hike from Weissenbach to Ischl—night, loneliness, pouring rain, hurry—and I tolerated it very well" (p. 92). It is fairly certain that the hike was to visit his mother, an expression of what Schur might have called "cordial filial duty." It may not be too far-fetched to consider this hike the expression of a reaction formation, the severity of the attendant conditions being a measure of the extreme hostility he defended against.

The repressed aggression that lay behind Freud's idealization of his mother has not gone undetected. Stolorow and Atwood (1978) write:

> . . . the positive, ambivalent-free quality of Freud's conscious attitudes toward his mother was the product of a defensive idealization process, serving to protect his image of their relationship from invasion by negative affects . . . this defensive idealization functioned ultimately to avert the dreaded emergence of murderous hostility toward her and ward off the catastrophic possibility of object loss. [pp. 218–219]

Dreams, however, are no respecters of idealization. In his seventh or eighth year Freud dreamed what he called a "true anxiety dream": . . . in it *I saw my beloved mother, with a peculiarly peaceful, sleeping expression on her features, being carried into the room by two (or three) people with birds' beaks and laid upon the bed.* I awoke in tears and screaming, and interrupted my parents' sleep (1900, 5:583 italics original). Freud interprets, after preliminary associations:

> The interpretation carried out in the dream by the "secondary revision" must therefore have been that my mother

> was dying; the funerary relief fitted in with this. I awoke in anxiety, which did not cease till I had woken my parents up. I remember that I suddenly grew calm when I saw my mother's face, as though I had needed to be reassured that she was not dead. . . . The anxiety can be traced back, when repression is taken into account, to an obscure and evidently sexual craving that had found appropriate expression in the visual content of the dream. [1900, pp. 583–584]

Groping for the origin and meaning of dreams during the early years of his discoveries, Freud wrote to Fliess: "Biologically, dream life seems to me to derive entirely from the residues of the prehistoric period of life (between the ages of one and three)—the same period which is the source of the unconscious and alone contains the etiology of all the psychoneuroses, the period normally characterized by an amnesia analogous to hysterical amnesia" (1985a, p. 302). Consistently, however, in his interpretation of dreams, Freud traces their derivation to the oedipal stage of development, ignoring the earlier, preoedipal period. So in this dream of his dying mother, he traces the anxiety back to a sexual craving in preference to his repressed, preoedipal rage. Interpreting the dream as the expression of his death wish against his mother, Stolorow and Atwood (1978) write: ". . . he retreats from such an interpretation and is at pains to show that the image of the dying mother is not a fulfillment of his aggressive wishes; rather he interprets it as an artifact of the dream-work and as concealing deeper, and, in this case, sexual wishes" (p. 223).

Stolorow and Atwood attribute Freud's aggressive feelings toward his mother to the continual arrival of siblings, rivals for her love. The birth of siblings engendered "the conflict between an intense possessive need for his mother's love and an equally intense, magically potent hatred" (1978, p. 222). But not all children who suffer the birth of siblings develop so intense a conflict. We would postulate that Freud's hatred for his mother, like his need for her love, predated the arrival of his siblings, their birth serving but to enhance feelings rooted in his earlier prehistory. From the very beginning, Freud must have felt the urgency of his mother's narcissistic need for him, and as the mother clung to her son, so did the son, perforce, cling to his mother, with love and with hate, repressing the hate and permitting only the love to see the light of day.

The question of Freud's reluctance to deal with aggression as a primary drive has long been a subject of speculation. Freud (1933) addressed this reluctance in himself: "Why have we ourselves needed such a long time before we decided to recognize an aggressive instinct? Why did we hesitate to make use, on behalf of our theory, of facts which were obvious and familiar to everyone? . . . it [the concept of an aggressive drive] contradicts too many religious presumptions and social conventions" (22:103–104). Freud did not hesitate to advance other concepts inimical to religious presumptions and social conventions. Why the hesitation now? Gay (1988) touches on what he sees as a factor that might explain Freud's reluctance:

> Most likely, his halting recognition [of aggression as a primary drive] also had a personal dimension; it may have been one of the self-protective defensive maneuvers he mobilized against his own aggressiveness. He blamed modern culture for rejecting the blasphemous low appraisal of human nature which made aggression a fundamental drive. Perhaps. But his own hesitation reads rather like a piece of projection in which he attributed to others his own denials. [p. 397]

Freud had no difficulty recognizing aggression when he saw it as reactive. If you hurt me, I react aggressively. But recognizing aggression as a primary force was another matter. Borrowing a page from Freud, who admittedly engaged in speculation in formulating the death instinct theory, let us engage in a bit of speculation of our own. Belatedly and reluctantly arriving at the concept of aggression as innate,

Freud sensed the possibility of becoming aware of his aggressive feelings toward his early mother. To defend against this dreaded realization he went on to postulate the concept of the death instinct, which turned the aggression inward. Only under the aegis of the death instinct was Freud able to accept the concept of an aggressive drive.

As Freud's idealization of his early mother is reflected in his conceptualizations, implicit in them as well is his warded off aggression. Gay (1988) deals with the impact of Freud's "hidden life" on his theoretical formulations in *Totem and Taboo*:

> . . . it is highly plausible that some of the impulses guiding Freud's argument in *Totem and Taboo* emerged from his hidden life . . . it is telling that in his reconstruction Freud said virtually nothing about the mother, even though the ethnographic material pointing to the fantasy of devouring the mother is richer than that for devouring the father. Ferenczi's little Arpad, whom Freud borrowed as a witness for *Totem and Taboo*, wanted to make a meal of his "*preserved mother*"; as he graphically put it, "One should put my mother into a pot and cook her, then there would be a preserved mother and I could eat her." But Freud chose to ignore this piece of evidence. [p. 335]

In like manner, Freud bypassed the mothers in his famous cases, exiling them, Gay (1988) points out, to the margins of his case histories.

> Dora's mother, beset by what Freud called a "housewife's psychosis," is a silent, minor actor in the family melodrama. Little Hans's mother, though to her husband's mind the cause of her son's neurosis with her seductive behavior, is subordinated to that husband. . . . The Wolf Man's biological mother achieves only severely limited significance. . . . The Rat Man's mother makes some fleeting appearances. . . .

> And Schreber's mother might as well not have lived. [p. 505]

Dealing with mothers might, by association, bring Freud perilously close to his own mother and his relationship with her.

In discussing the child's aggression toward the mother, it is in keeping with his need to idealize that Freud points to the girl as being the child who retains her hostility toward her first object.

> We will now turn our interest on to the single question of what it is that brings this powerful attachment of the girl to her mother to an end. This, as we know, is its usual fate: it is destined to make room for an attachment to her father. . . . The turning away from the mother is accomplished by hostility; the attachment to the mother ends in hate. [1933, 22:121]

As for the boy: ". . . boys are able to deal with their ambivalent feelings toward their mother by directing all their hostility on to their father" (1931a, 21:235). Furthermore:

> The evidence of psychoanalysis shows that every intimate emotion between two people . . . contains a sediment of feelings of aversion and hostility. . . . Footnote: Perhaps with the solitary exception of the relation of a mother to her son, which is based on narcissism, and is reinforced by a rudimentary attempt at sexual-object choice. [1921, 18:101]

Thus mother and son are alike absolved of feelings of aggression toward each other.

"I cannot think of any need in childhood," Freud wrote in *Civilization and Its Discontents*, "as strong as the need for a father's protection" (1930, 21:72). For the oedipal child, perhaps. But Freud ignores an earlier and far stronger childhood need—the need for the mother's protection. How explain this oversight? The forcefulness of Freud's statement, contrasting sharply with his more characteristic open-ended formulations, suggests an emotional component. The protection Freud sorely needed was not by his mother. What he longed for was protection by his father against the engulfing tendencies of his mother. But here his father had failed him, abandoning him to his mother and leaving him no recourse but to consign his rage to the unconscious, layering it over with denial and idealization. "Man is afraid of woman," Marie Bonaparte once observed to Freud. "He's right," Freud responded (Gay 1988, p. 522). Could Freud have been afraid of his mother?

2

KEEP WELL FOR YOUR SIGMUND

> Childhood love is boundless; it demands exclusive possession. It is not content with less than all.
>
> Even a marriage is not made secure until the wife has succeeded in making her husband her child as well as in acting like a mother to him.
>
> —Freud

On a spring evening in 1882, Freud returned home from his work at Brücke's Institute and was proceeding to his room, when a glance at the people gathered around the family table brought him to a halt. Seated there was a visitor, a young woman—petite, dark-haired, dark-eyed, animated, peeling an apple as she chatted with his sisters. To the amazement and perhaps the amusement of the family members, instead of going on to his room as he usually did, regardless of who might be visiting, Freud joined the circle. This was in April, a few weeks before Freud's twenty-sixth birthday. Martha Bernays, the visitor, was five years his junior. The two were secretly engaged the following month.

Without the money to marry, he working at research in Brücke's laboratory and uncertain of how, or even where, he would make a living necessary to support a family, and she without a dowry to cushion the early years of marriage, the engagement dragged on for more than four years. And for more than three of these four years, Martha, her mother, and her sister Minna, lived in Wandsbek, a suburb of Hamburg, where the sisters had been born and where their mother found living more congenial than in Vienna. Unable to see each other for months on end, and with only an occasional visit when Freud could scrape together enough money to take the trip to Wandsbek, the two wrote letters, almost daily. After Freud's death Martha wanted to burn the letters, but yielding to her daughter Anna's appeal, they were spared, and the ninety-three letters that were published of the nine hundred Freud had written provide not only a vivid account of his environment and activities in Vienna, his research, family concerns, and sketches of his colleagues and friends, but also vividly evoke the tenor of the relationship. Most revealing, perhaps, of the depth of his yearning for Martha during the long period of waiting is Freud's fantasy of an ideal marriage:

> Oh, my darling Marty, how poor we are! Suppose we were to tell the world we are planning to share life and they were to ask us: What is your dowry?—Nothing but our love for each other.—Nothing else?—Now it occurs to me that we would need two or three little rooms to live and eat in and to receive a guest, and a stove in which the fire for our meals never goes out. And just think of all the things that have got to go into the rooms! Tables and chairs, beds, mirrors, a clock to remind the happy couple of the passage of time, an armchair for an hour's pleasant daydreaming, carpets to help the housewife keep the floors clean, linen tied with pretty ribbons in the cupboard and dresses of the latest fashion and hats with artificial flowers, pictures on the wall,

> glasses for everyday and others for wine and festive occasions, plates and dishes, a small larder in case we are suddenly attacked by hunger or a guest, and an enormous bunch of keys—which must make a rattling noise. And there will be so much to enjoy, the books and the sewing table and the cozy lamp, and everything must be kept in good order or else the housewife, who has divided her heart into little bits, one for each piece of furniture, will begin to fret. And this object must bear witness to the serious work that holds the household together, that object to a feeling for beauty, to dear friends one likes to remember, to cities one has visited, to hours one wants to recall. And all this, a small world of happiness, of silent friends and proofs of lofty human values, is as yet only in the future; not even the foundation of the house has been laid, there is nothing but two poor human creatures who love one another to distraction. [1960, p. 27]

Here was paradise deferred, life with mother, who was to be exclusively his. It is somewhat difficult to picture the young research scholar, the conquistador, as he would one day see himself, one destined to disturb the sleep of the world, carefully, with childlike precision, detailing the furnishings of the "two or three little rooms to live and eat in and to receive a guest." There is great emphasis, in the fantasy, on food, of vital concern to a young child, and on the accoutrements necessary for its preparation and consumption. The larder, like the rooms, is small, enough to accommodate mother and child, and perhaps an occasional guest; the fire in the stove (symbol for mother) never goes out. Although guests are given a perfunctory nod of welcome at the beginning of the fantasy, nothing more is heard of them except as "silent friends" and "dear friends one likes to remember," but should a guest make an appearance, he is seen, curiously, as an "attack," like hunger.

The child's demand for exclusivity is a motif that runs like a turbulent stream through the letters. Martha is to be his alone. "I know you have not misunderstood my efforts to make you my own as intimately as possible, and if this be egotistical, love after all cannot be anything but egotistical" (1960, p. 25). In the exclusivity of their relationship, he expected that she turn to him alone for advice, instruction, or even for some physical necessity. "Should you need something from here or want something done, please don't favor anyone but me with your commissions. That is how exclusive I am when I love" (1960, p. 9). One winter in Wandsbek, Martha asks for permission to go ice-skating. Freud refuses to grant it, not, as Jones (who fortunately had access to all the letters) wryly observes, "from fear of her breaking her leg but because it might necessitate her being arm in arm with another man. . . . He was, however, not quite sure on the point, so he asked his friend Paneth for a ruling. Three days later he granted permission, but on condition that she skate unaccompanied" (1953, pp. 133–134).

Fritz Wahle, an artist, a close friend of Freud, and, in the words of Jones, a "brotherly friend" of Martha, was suspected by Freud of having more than brotherly feelings for his loved one, although engaged to Martha's cousin Elise. Artists, in Freud's view—at least at that stressful period of his life—had a way with women, and Wahle, he had been told, was able to coax any woman away from another man (hardly a compliment to Martha, who, it is to be inferred, could not be trusted to know her own mind). "I think there is a general enmity between artists and those engaged in the details of scientific work. We know that they possess in their art a master key to open with ease all female hearts, whereas we stand helpless at the strange design of the lock and have first to torment ourselves to discover a suitable key to it" (Jones 1953, p. 111). For a long time Martha resisted Freud's demands that she end her relationship with Wahle; eventually his jealousy prevailed, and Martha gave way. The memory of the past, however, continued to rankle painfully.

> There was one instance in which you were not quite fair to me and offended me deeply; it was when you refused to drop your "friendship" with Fritz Wahle for my sake. I was patient and finally you did do me justice. And even at the time I was fully conscious that you nobly kept your independence and truthfully reported everything to me. You will eventually agree with me more fully on this point. You were not quite sure enough in your judgment; let us both hope that such things will never happen between us again. And you will understand me when I say that even for a beloved girl there is still one further step up: to that of friend, and that it would be a ghastly loss for us both if I were compelled to decide to love you as a dear girl, yet not as an equal, someone from whom I would have to hide my thoughts and opinions—in short, the truth. [1960, pp. 29–30]

Freud here presents his "beloved girl" with a dilemma. On the one hand, he commends her for her independence, which he acknowledges to be noble; on the other hand, he asks that she give up her independence and do as he wishes when the result of carrying her independence into practice displeases him. Freud writes earlier in the letter, "You know that from the moment we entered into this alliance we both had to change to some extent in order to become for each other what we wish to be, and perhaps I may be allowed to say and to explain when the old Marty does not seem to have given way completely to my beloved girl" (1960, p. 29). In other words, they must each change to some extent, the "some extent" being for Marty that she give way completely to what he would like her to be. Marty must indeed have been a most loving and understanding soul.

Not only, in order to satisfy her lover's desire for exclusivity, must Martha renounce her friendship with men of whom he does not approve, but she must extend this to people who have caused him distress, specifically, her brother Eli, and most particularly, her mother, "whose heartlessness and caprice [in removing Martha to Wandsbek] I hold responsible for your departure." On one occasion, Freud, finding the separation unbearable, presented a plan for having his friend Fleischl-Marxow find employment for Martha in Vienna. For Freud, Martha's coming to Vienna would not only bring her closer to him, but would have the additional merit of removing her from her mother's influence. Martha, responding favorably to the plan, saw in it yet another merit: her coming to Vienna would relieve her mother of the burden of supporting her, and until employment could be found, she would stay with her brother Eli. Poor Martha. She had put a match to a powder keg. As if the reason for her coming to Vienna was to relieve her mother! She had put her mother's interests before him! ". . . according to that, it would be the same if you went to Hungary. . . . If that is so, you are my enemy; if we don't get over this obstacle we shall founder. You have only an Either-Or. If you can't be fond enough of me to renounce your family, then you must lose me, wreck my life, and not get much yourself out of your family" (Jones 1953, p. 130). "Once more," Jones remarks, "Martha's tact and sweetness succeeded in smoothing things over . . ." (p. 130).

Freud's outbursts, when they occurred, were eruptions not only from his well of loneliness and his ungratified need for Martha. "Since I am violent and passionate with all sorts of devils pent up that cannot emerge, they rumble about inside or else are released against you, you dear one. Had I only some daring activity where I could venture and win, I should be gentle at home, but I am forced to exercise moderation and self-control, and I even enjoy a reputation for doing so" (Jones 1953, pp. 195–196). Fortunately, Freud at last found a daring activity where his pent up devils found release. But no doubt haunting him, and adding to his discontent in the days of his courtship, was the specter of his father's improvidence. Would he, like Jakob, be unable to provide adequately for his family? Even years later, the fear of poverty persisted. The father of six, on the eve of the appearance of his dream book, he wrote to Fliess: "My mood also depends very strongly on my earnings. Money is laughing gas for me. I know from my youth that once the wild horses of the pampas have been lassoed, they retain a certain anxiousness for life. Thus I came to know the helplessness of poverty and continually fear it" (1985a, p. 374). How much greater must have been the anxiety and fear during the four years that preceded his marriage. Since Martha was the woman who would be his wife and mother of his children for whom he must provide, and since it was for their sake he had left his research in Brücke's Institute where he had spent "the happiest years of my youth" and entered the General Hospital for the clinical experience necessary to become a physician, "against my will," Martha, though loved and cherished, could not help but be an unwitting object of his unconscious resentment.

That Martha belong exclusively to him, Freud pointed out to her, was not mere willfulness on his part. Exclusivity of wife to husband had been hallowed by tradition. "For has it not been laid down since time immemorial that the woman should leave father and mother and follow the man she has chosen? You must not take it too hard, Marty, you cannot fight against it; no matter how much they love you, I will not leave you to anyone, and no one deserves you; no one else's love compares with mine" (1960, p. 23). But Freud goes beyond what has been laid down since time immemorial. Not only is Martha expected to leave father and mother and follow the man she has chosen, but she must share his hostility for her mother (her father is dead) and for her brother Eli as well. (Minna, her younger sister, of whom he approved, perhaps partly because she was critical of her mother, was excluded from those in her family she must renounce for his sake.)

Exclusivity extended to matters other than belonging solely to him and sharing his attitudes, likes, and dislikes. He would like her to send him a photograph of herself, if possible life size "to consecrate my new room . . . and if I am the only one to receive a picture from you, I shall be especially happy" (1960, p. 93). Nor was the stationery she used to write to him to be used in her correspondence with others. "I wanted exclusiveness and since I have attained it in great and important matters, I strove to achieve it in small and symbolic ones. . . . So I decided to acquire some notepaper for the dear industrious child and chose some on which she could write to me only. An M and an S intimately entwined . . . renders every page useless for intercourse save between Marty and me" (1960, p. 18).

Time and again Freud insists that there be no secrets between them, that their thinking be not only shared, but in complete accord, "Goodnight, my dearest little woman, keep pouring out your heart to me. I feel so sad when you haven't done so for some time" (1960, p. 72). Jones (1953) comments on the extremity of Freud's possessiveness in regard to Martha: "Their relationship must be quite perfect; the slightest blur was not to be tolerated. At times it seems as if his goal was fusion rather than union" (p. 110). Which, on an unconscious level, was precisely Freud's goal: fusion with the early mother, to whom Martha was surrogate.

Considering Freud's insistence that Martha subordinate her attitudes and opinions to his, it is edifying to read: "I am quite prepared to be completely ruled by my princess. One willingly lets oneself be dominated by the person one loves . . ." (1960, p. 51). Behind the sound and fury was the yearning to be dominated, to be the child of a mother whose sole interest and concern would be his well-being. This was to put himself back in time to his infancy, when life depended entirely on mother's dominance and ministrations. "Let us not despise the times when for me a day was made worth living merely by a letter from you, when a decision from you meant a decision between life and death" (1960, p. 133). Here Martha is endowed with the omnipotence of the mother on whom the child's survival depends.

Since, for the young child, survival depends on mother's

love and care, she must at all times be strong and healthy. It is therefore not surprising to read in Freud's letters to Martha—a completely strong and healthy young woman—constant expressions of concern about her health. "Long may she remain this way and healthy to boot" (1960, p. 47). "With best wishes for my little princess's health . . ." (1960, p. 103). And, of course, long before their marriage, he indicated that if they remained in Vienna he would get for her the best family doctor the city boasted: Joseph Breuer. "Now please write to me as much about yourself as I have of myself. And also whether you are well, completely well. Whether the iron is doing you good and whether you are drinking any wine. I shall be angry if you don't say yes to both" (1960, p. 109). Even when there is no cause for concern, he persists in his concern. "I can see quite clearly from your letters that you are well, but please tell me what you look like, whether you have put on weight, whether you are feeling better and if your complexion is clearer than when you left. . . . And what about the cold baths; is it again too cold for them?" (1960, p. 56). When Frau Bernays was at one time ill, Freud was concerned, not about her, but about Martha, who was nursing her. "Don't you at least take turns with Minna and go into the air a little? Marty, if you get ill over this I shall make a big fuss and you will see that it is not only patients but also lovers who can be egoistic" (1960, p. 106). Minna's fiancé, Schönberg, who was also a friend of Freud, was severely ill with tuberculosis (of which he eventually died). After visiting the Bernays in Wandsbek he returned to Vienna.

> Schönberg let one word slip out which hurt me very much. He told me . . . that she [Martha] looked well but had "dark rings under her eyes"—Why has my little woman dark rings under her eyes? From that moment my spirits fell and all the selfishness of a human being revealed itself by my being much more shaken by your dark rings than by the poor man's deplorable condition. [1960, p. 167]

It has been suggested that Freud's constant concern about Martha's health would indicate a defense against hostile feelings. But this view would not seem in accord with his barely concealed concern about himself, should Martha fall ill. "Farewell," he concludes one of his letters, "and keep well for your Sigmund" (1960, p. 84). "Keep well for your Sigmund" was the crux of his concern, the expression of his need for a mother's love and protection. The intensity of his fear when Martha was ill, or when he suspected that she was ill, suggests the most primitive of early fears: loss of the object. "I really get quite beside myself when I am disturbed about you. I lose at once all sense of values, and at moments a frightful dread comes over me lest you fall ill. I am so wild that I can't write much more" (Jones 1953, p. 132). The next day, after hearing from Martha: "So I was quite wrong in imagining you to be ill. I was very crazy. One is very crazy when one is in love" (Jones 1953, p. 132). Or when one is a young child and there looms the fear of losing mother. On a holiday at Lübeck, Martha had a fantasy of drowning, of which she wrote to Freud. His reply: "There must be a point of view from which even the loss of the loved one would seem a trivial occurrence in the thousands of years of human history. But I must confess I take the extreme opposite one in which the event would be absolutely equivalent to the end of the world, at least the world as far as I am concerned" (Jones 1953, p. 132).

The approach of his marriage seemed to intensify Freud's concern about Martha's health. Her falling ill at so crucial a moment in his life would be the last straw. In June, several months preceding the wedding, Freud sent Martha a sum of money with instructions that it be used solely to take a holiday. "If I find you have spent it on a garment I will tear it up when I come, and if I don't know which it is I will tear them all up" (Jones 1953, p. 146). No doubt written in jest, but nonetheless reflecting his concern.

In another letter Freud gives a chilling description of the feeling of elemental orality he experienced after suffering a severe angina of the throat which prevented his swallowing or speaking for several days. Upon recovering, "he was seized with 'a gigantic hunger like an animal waking from a winter sleep.' This was followed by an intense longing for his beloved: 'a frightful yearning—frightful is hardly the right word, better would be uncanny, ghastly, gigantic; in short, an indescribable longing for you' " (Jones 1953, p. 169). If such is the ferocity of the longing of the young infant for its mother, it is indeed fortunate that it is helpless.

It is no easy matter, reading Freud's letters, to see the real Martha. Was she a docile, compliant Martha? Freud accused her of not strongly enough opposing the move to Wandsbek, of being too compliant to the dictates of her mother, the "enemy" of their love, or was she a stubborn, self-willed Martha who refused for too long to give up her friendship with Wahle or to renounce mother and brother for her lover's sake? It would seem that in the essentials, in what she saw as principles, she could stand her ground. She could not be brought to renounce her mother and brother, realizing, no doubt, that there would be accommodations on both sides, as indeed there were. In finally giving up her friendship with Wahle, the source of real misery to Freud, she gave way, unfounded though she knew his jealousy to be. Jones, from his own observations, describes Martha as sweet, gracious, devoted. "But, as Freud was painfully to discover, she was not at heart docile and she had a firmness of character that did not readily lend itself to being molded" (Jones 1953, p. 102). ". . . she had in addition something very tough and spirited in her personality and when forced to an issue, an art in which Freud was accomplished, she could stand up for herself with even greater tenacity than he could maintain" (Jones 1953, pp. 121–122). And Freud's own assessment of Martha: ". . . so sure of herself, so reticent, so gently decided in her opinions and inclinations" (Jones 1953, p. 126).

It is doubtful that Freud was "painfully to discover" that Martha was not docile. Knowing her for more than four years he could not but be aware that his "dear little woman" who asked his permission to go ice-skating was submissive only when minor issues were at stake, when to be submissive best served the harmony of their relationship. So that, his protests and outcries notwithstanding, Freud wanted her as she was. Her firmness would be the influence necessary to check his own unreasonable demands. "For a long, long time I have criticized you and picked you to pieces, and the result of it all is that I want nothing but to have you, and have you just as you are" (1960, p. 201). Freud no doubt sensed that Martha had the strength of character to contend with his passions and the devils pent up in him. His instinct for self-preservation drew him to a woman diametrically opposed to his volatile, demanding mother. Some years later, Freud referred to ". . . her extremely reserved nature" in a letter to Fliess (1985a, p. 50). "My mother," Martin Freud (1958) wrote of Martha, "shared my father's ability to control her emotions" (p. 38). An ability Amalia did not possess.

"Do you remember," Freud (1960) wrote to Martha some two years into their engagement,

> how you often used to tell me that I had a talent for repeatedly provoking your resistance? How we were always fighting, and you would never give in to me? We were two people who diverged in every detail of life and who were yet determined to love each other, and did love each other. . . . I found you so fully matured and every corner in you occupied, and you were hard and reserved and I had no power over you. This resistance of yours only made you the more precious to me. . . . [p. 117]

The lack Freud felt in himself ("I cannot mature properly") he found compensated for in Martha. In this young woman five years his junior and without his intellectual endowments, he encountered a fully integrated personality, so well grounded in her own identity that she would have no need or desire for invasion. Freud theorized in later years: "A man, especially, looks for someone who can represent his picture of his mother, as it has dominated his mind from his earliest childhood . . ." (1905, 7:228). Unless, of course, one seeks to flee from the mother who has dominated his mind from his earliest childhood. Flight from Amalia brought him to Martha.

The cozy nest Freud had hoped for Martha provided, though expanded in time to contain six children and, from the mid-nineties, his sister-in-law Minna as well. Married in September, 1886, Freud was able to write to his friend Carl Keller the following month: "My little wife, with the help of her dowry [a gift from a relative] and wedding presents has made a charming home" (1985b, p. 131). And the "little wife," instinctively responding to her husband's need, became his mother as well. No matter the slings and arrows of the outside world when his devils emerged and he forged ahead with his discoveries, his home was his sanctuary. "I always tried as much as possible," Martha wrote after her husband's death in response to a letter of condolence from Binswanger, "to remove from his path the *misère* of everyday life" (Binswanger 1957, p. 102). How well she succeeded is attested to by visitor after visitor to Berggasse 19. Freud's famous patient, the Wolf Man (1971), found that "everything here contributed to one's feeling of leaving the haste of modern life behind, of being sheltered from one's daily care" (p. 139). Laforgue (1956) recalled Martha as a "practical woman, marvelously skillful in creating an atmosphere of peace and *joie de vivre*. Moreover, she was an excellent housewife, a rather rare phenomenon in a milieu as here" (p. 342). From Pfister (Freud and Pfister 1963) to Martha, after Freud's death, perhaps a bit hyperbolic:

> In your house one felt as in a sunny spring garden, heard the gay song of larks and blackbirds, saw bright flower-beds, and had a premonition of the rich blessing of summer. To the visitor it was immediately evident that a large part of

> that blessing was to be attributed to you, and that you with your gentle, kindly nature, kept putting fresh weapons into your husband's hands in the fierce battle of life. . . . and without you even the giant that he was would have been unable to achieve the tremendous task on behalf of good-for-nothing humanity that his life-work represents. [pp. 145–146]

Thanks to Martha's management, everything in the large household revolved around Freud: his routine, his needs, his comfort and convenience. ". . . at the stroke of one," writes Martin, "everybody in the household was seated at the long dining-room table and at the same moment one door opened to let the maid enter with the soup while another door opened to allow my father to walk in from his study to take his place at the head of the table facing my mother at the other end" (M. Freud 1958, pp. 32–33). One might speculate that there was something in Freud that induced in Martha the urge to mother him, and that he, in a sense, was her favorite child. "Though fond of the opera, she [Martha] never managed to come in time to hear the overture, although the opera house was close by on the Berggasse, because that was the time Freud had his dinner" (Reik 1971, p. 80). This, despite the fact that there was a housekeeper and three daughters willing and able to take her place. "She laid out his clothes, chose everything for him down to his handkerchiefs, and even put toothpaste on his toothbrush" (Roazen 1976, pp. 56–57). Parsimony having been a "grim necessity" in the early days of her marriage, Martha retained the habit of careful expenditure "in everything that did not concern father" (M. Freud 1958, p. 93). "My mother, who ordered all my father's clothes, tried to reach absolute perfection, always taking the greatest care in ordinary well-cut clothes made from British cloth" (M. Freud 1958, p. 125). Traveling to the country for their summer holiday before the family could afford comfortable railroad accommodations proved a challenge which, Martin believed,

Martha "enjoyed meeting." Thanks to Alexander Freud's connection with the railroad establishment, the Freuds were able to get a third-class compartment for themselves. But all the furnishings this compartment could offer were hard wooden benches. However,

> with the help of rugs, cushions and pillows [mother] turned the shabby place into luxurious sleeping-quarters with quite a home atmosphere. . . . My father would have joined in willingly, but what was a victorious battle to my mother would have been, she knew, an ordeal to him; and she always arranged, possibly by subtle means unknown to us, to make him travel alone and in comfort. [M. Freud 1958, p. 44].

Concerned chiefly with her children, with running her large household efficiently, and with providing the conditions necessary to her husband for his work, Martha had little knowledge of, and perhaps little interest in, the significance of his discoveries and their impact on the world. According to Reik (personal communication), it was not until Freud's seventieth birthday, when the post offices of Vienna were kept open solely to deal with the influx of congratulatory letters and telegrams he received from around the world, that Martha became aware of the extent of her husband's fame. Her role of wife and mother was total, leaving her time for little else.

Writers on Freud have been puzzled by Martha's lack of interest in her husband's work. Freud discussed his work with other women: his daughter Anna, his sister-in-law Minna, Marie Bonaparte, Lou Andreas-Salomé. . . . Why not with his wife? Perhaps because she *was* his wife. Discussion of ideas might have seemed alien to Freud in a relationship whose emotional level was in part that of mother-child. What appeared to matter to Freud and apparently to Martha was not that she realize his importance to the world, but that she realize her importance to him. And what was important to Freud was apparently a wife who would function efficiently in her sphere, as he saw it. Andreas-Salomé noted after a visit with the Freuds:

> I . . . admired Frau Freud's ability to fulfill her part unerringly in things that concerned her. She was always devoted and always ready to make decisions, but she did not take it upon herself to interfere in tasks which she considered her husband's. . . . It was doubtless through her that the upbringing of their six children remained remote from psychoanalysis, yet this was certainly not due to any indifference on Freud's part. But he did derive a certain satisfaction, I now see, in knowing that his domestic circle was far removed from any public conflict and his wife's part in this was a source of pleasure to him. (Freud and Andreas-Salomé 1972, p. 230)

Apparently, more important to Freud than a wife with whom he could discuss his ideas was a wife who was able to create a serene, pressure-free atmosphere in which he could develop his ideas. Did Freud, during his stormy courtship, have an intimation of what his future life with Martha would be? "You give me not only aim and direction, but so much happiness as well that I cannot be dissatisfied with the otherwise rather wretched present; you give me hope and certainty of success. I knew it before you loved me and I know now that you do love me and it is your doing that I have become a self-confident, courageous man" (1960, p. 57).

It is possible, too, that Freud was unable to blend the attributes of the intellectual woman with those of the motherly woman. Or perhaps he could not see the intellectual woman as also being motherly. So that for him a separation of the two might, in fact, have been necessary. ". . . it might perhaps be fair to describe his view of the female sex as having as their main function to be ministering angels to the needs and comforts of man," writes Jones (1955). "His letters and his love choice make it plain that he had only one type of sexual object in his mind, a gentle, feminine one" (p. 421). Jones's assessment of Freud's view of the woman's role is confirmed in one of Freud's letters to his daughter Mathilde: "The more intelligent among young men are sure to know what to look for in a wife—gentleness, cheerfulness, and the talent to make their life easier and more beautiful" (Freud 1960, p. 272).

As mother is central to the child's world before he has learned to separate and create a world of his own, so was Martha for Freud. When separated from her, he felt removed from the source of his security. A day without a letter from Martha during his courtship was a day of misery. He had agreed with Martha that in the winter, when the weather was bad, she might write every other day instead of every day "so as to get some exercise." "But Marty," he cautioned her, "you will then have to write a little more every other day, otherwise I might develop an uncontrollable hunger for news of you" (1960, p. 55). Freud's need for closeness with mother did not lessen even after years of marriage. Whether at home with Martha or embarked on one of his tours, she remained the focal point toward which he gravitated. Busy with her household responsibilities and unequal to Freud's rapid and restless pace, she was not always able to accompany him on his travels. But whether alone or with a companion, he sent her daily a postcard or a telegram, and every few days a long letter reporting on all he had seen and done. To keep in constant touch with her was a necessity; breaking the bond set him adrift.

The *"grande passion"*—as Jones terms Freud's feelings for Martha during their engagement—did not include grand sexuality. It is ironic that the man who is familiar to most people for his espousal of greater sexual freedom should have been so little interested in sexuality in his personal life. "I stand for an infinitely freer sexual life," he wrote to Putnam, "although I myself have made very little use of such freedom" (1960, p. 308). Nor did he suffer gladly his own emphasis on the sexual factor in the etiology of neurosis. Defensively, it would seem, he points to others who came upon the discovery before him.

> I will only remark that the singling out of the sexual factor in the etiology of hysteria springs at least from no preconceived opinion on my part. The two investigators as whose pupil I began my studies of hysteria, Charcot and Breuer, were far from having any such predisposition; in fact, they had a personal disinclination to it which I originally shared. [1896, 3:189]

And which he may have continued to share to such a degree that even when convinced of the validity of his discovery of infantile sexuality, he wrote, in a revealing parapraxis: "Though we think highly of the happiness of childhood because it is still innocent of sexual desires . . ." (1900, 4:130). When the slip was pointed out to him, Freud corrected the error in a footnote in a later edition, but let it stand in the text. It is interesting too that he equates happiness with freedom from sexual desires. In a letter to Jones, Freud gave what he perceived to be the reason for the more favorable reception accorded Jung's presentation of psychoanalysis, which glossed over the concept of sexuality: "Anyone who promises to mankind liberation from hardship of sex will be hailed as a hero, let him talk whatever nonsense he chooses" (Jones 1955, p. 151). Did Freud see sex as a hardship? Jones remarks again and again on Freud's sexual disposition as he saw it: "his personal puritanical predilections," "the chaste and puritanical Freud," "his unusually great sexual repression."

> Freud was quite peculiarly monogamous. Of few men can it be said that they go through the whole of life without being erotically moved in any serious fashion by any woman beyond the one and only one. Yet this seems to have been true of Freud. . . . Such men are fortunate indeed if all goes well with the great choice, as happened to Freud, but whether they are to be regarded as representing the true

> normality of males is a question that only social or psychological anthropology can answer. [1955, pp. 421–422]

Jones (1955) conjectures that "... it is likely that the more passionate side of married life subsided with him [Freud] earlier than it does with many men" (p. 386). When he was forty-one, Freud wrote to Fliess that "sexual excitation is of no more use to a person like me" (1954, p. 227). Three years later: "You know how limited my pleasures are. I must not smoke heavy cigars ... I have finished with begetting children, and I am cut off from contact with people" (1954, p. 312). And to Jung, when he was fifty-four: "My Indian summer of eroticism that we spoke of on our trip has withered lamentably under the pressure of work. I am resigned to being old and no longer even think continually of growing old" (Freud and Jung 1974, p. 292). A prime example of sublimation. In his *Psychopathology of Everyday Life*, published when he was forty-five, Freud recounts an experience of his own with a young girl who "aroused a feeling of pleasure in me which I had long thought was extinct" (1901, 6:175). It is likely that part of the sexual energy that would be expected to flow into the oedipal state, remained, for Freud, arrested at the preoedipal stage of development.

"The great question that has never been answered," Freud declared to Marie Bonaparte, "and which I have not yet been able to answer, despite my thirty years of research into the feminine soul, is 'What does a woman want?' " (Jones 1955, p. 421). If the yield of Freud's thirty years of research into the feminine soul was that "the sexual life of adult women is a 'dark continent' for psychology" (1927, 20:212), then we must question the intensity of the research. In far less than thirty years Freud brought light to other dark continents. Why the impenetrability of this particular area of research? Perhaps probing too deeply into the question of what a woman wants would have meant confronting the question of what he, Freud, wanted in his relationship with a woman. To avoid exploration of his relationship with his early mother, woman, for Freud, was destined to remain a dark continent.

In his paper, "The Theme of the Three Caskets," Freud saw woman in man's life in three guises: the mother who bore him, his mate and mother of his children, and Mother Earth, who embraces him in death. Woman in her role of mate was not of prime importance to Freud. He gave up sex at a relatively early age, fortunately sublimating along channels that have greatly enriched our culture. This left the other guises as the important ones, the mother who bore him and Mother Earth, who represents death. "But it is in vain that an old man yearns for the love of woman as he had it first from his mother; the third of the Fates alone, the silent Goddess of Death, will take him into her arms" (1913, 12:301).

In a letter written to Freud in 1911, when he was fifty-five, Emma Jung refers to a conversation she had had with him: "You said then that your marriage had long been 'amortized,' now there was nothing more to do except—die" (Freud and Jung 1974, p. 456). Having fathered six children, Freud saw his man's responsibility as over. For the rest, he must wait for the silent Goddess of Death to take him into her arms.

3

I WENT TO SEE BREUER

> My emotional life has always insisted that I should have an intimate friend and a hated enemy. I have always been able to provide myself afresh with both and it has not infrequently happened . . . that friend and enemy have come together in a single individual—though not, of course, both at once or with constant oscillation.
>
> —Freud

Freud entered the University of Vienna in 1873, at the age of seventeen. The course of studies for a medical degree generally took approximately five years. But it was not until eight years later, when he was twenty-five, that Freud was graduated and received his medical degree. Considering his poverty and the pressing need to make a living, what was it that made Freud close his eyes to reality, pursuing only half-heartedly the courses necessary for his degree and seizing, in Jones's words, "every opportunity to dally in those that interested him as well as to forage in neighboring fields" (1953, p. 61)? The truth was, Freud quickly discovered, that he did not relish the idea of being a physician, and from the moment he received his degree he contemplated "with an increasingly heavy heart" the necessity of leaving his neurological research and entering the field of medicine. With a strong aversion to dealing with diseases and illnesses and with as strong a penchant for scientific research, it was in Brücke's Physiological Institute that Freud chose to dally for six years. Here, he wrote later in his *Autobiographical Study*, "I found rest and full satisfaction" (1925, 20:9). And here he would have been happy to remain, contentedly working on problems of the nervous system set before him by his revered Brücke and hoping one day to make a discovery that would lead to acclaim and obviate the need to be a doctor of medicine. Though twice coming close to making such a discovery, this was not to be. In 1882 Freud met Martha, and the need to make a living became urgent. The position of Demonstrator at the Institute, to which he had been promoted, paying but a pittance, and the hope of becoming an Assistant being a possibility only in the remote future (Brücke already had two satisfactory Assistants), Freud, on Brücke's advice, left the Institute and entered the Vienna General Hospital for the clinical experience necessary for private practice.

It was at Brücke's Institute that Freud met the man who was to lead him to the brink of what was to become for Freud the passionate preoccupation of his life: the subterranean world of the unconscious. Fourteen years Freud's senior, Josef Breuer had not only made several important physiological discoveries by the time of their meeting, but was also one of the most highly regarded and sought-after internists in Vienna, a "doctor's doctor," personal physician to many of the eminent in the professional community, among them Brücke himself. Warm-hearted, gregarious, widely cultured in areas other than those of his professional interests, Breuer was drawn to the young scientist in search of a future. "He was a man of striking intelligence," Freud wrote of Breuer years later in his *Autobiographical Study*. "Our relations soon became more intimate and he became my friend and helper in my difficult circumstances. We grew accustomed to share all our scientific interests with each other. In this relationship the gain was naturally mine" (1925, p. 19).

Torn with a hundred indecisions, whether to struggle on in the hope of achieving recognition as a scientist, whether to remain in Vienna where the likelihood of making a living seemed slim, whether to become a physician skilled in setting broken bones and helping in childbirth and so be more certain of security, whether to migrate to England, America, Australia, to some provincial town or perhaps even to the moon, Freud found himself turning more and more for advice and consolation to Breuer, his understanding and sympathetic friend. To report a success, to deplore a failure, to discuss an issue, the road invariably led to Breuer. "I went to see Breuer" became a constant refrain in Freud's letters to Martha. "Yesterday, in my joy [over the success of an experiment] I went to see Breuer" (1960, p. 71). "Afterwards . . . I went to see Breuer . . . so as to recover from my disappointment. They [Breuer and his wife Mathilde] are dear, good, and understanding friends. . . . We talked till 1 A.M . . ." (1960, p. 112). "It is four years today since I got my doctor's degree, and I celebrated the occasion by doing nothing and paying a call on Breuer . . ." (1960, p. 139). Perhaps one of the most memorable of Freud's visits to his friend was the one paid on a hot summer night, when the conversation turned to a patient of Breuer who came to be celebrated as Anna O.

> Today was the hottest, most excruciating day of the whole season, I was really almost crazy with exhaustion. Realizing that I was badly in need of refreshment, I went to see Breuer, from whom I have just returned, rather late. He had a headache, the poor man, and was taking salicyl. The first thing he did was to chase me into the bathtub, which I left rejuvenated. . . . Then we had supper upstairs in our shirt-sleeves . . . and then came a lengthy medical conversation on moral insanity and nervous diseases and strange case histo-

> ries—your friend Bertha Pappenheim [Anna O.] also cropped up—and then we became rather personal and very intimate and he told me a number of things about his wife and children and asked me to repeat what he had said only "after you are married to Martha." [1960, pp. 40–41]

So close did the friendship between the two men become that Freud often accompanied Breuer on his rounds, which, at times, would take them beyond the confines of Vienna and they would be obliged to spend the night at an inn. On at least one such occasion, in order to spare Freud the necessity of tipping the waiter—an amenity he could ill afford—Breuer entered his friend's name as his brother in the *Gasthaus* book. And once, unforgettable to one whose forays into the country were still a dream of the future, Freud spent several days in a summer house the Breuers had rented in Gmunden in the Salzkammergut. "Freud had never been so far from Vienna," Jones (1953) reports, "or gazed at such beautiful scenery, and he wrote a long lyrical account of this wonderful experience" (p. 168). Like a member of the Breuer family, Freud came and went at will. "Finding no one at home, I settled down in the consulting room and picked up the nearest book—I looked in vain for the cigar box (I have been granted these rights once and for all.)" (Freud 1960, p. 72). And for Freud, the right to the cigar box was an important one indeed.

Sensitive to the flaws and virtues of his fellow men, Freud (1960) found no difficulty finding words of praise for Breuer, "the ever-loyal Breuer," "he radiates light and warmth," "he is a man who always understands one," "saying only good things about him one doesn't give a proper picture of his character; one ought to emphasize the absence of so many bad things" (p. 149). And words of praise from Breuer were manna, to be shared with Martha:

> You know what Breuer told me one evening? I was so moved by what he said that in return I disclosed to him the

> secret of our engagement. He told me that he had discovered that hidden under the surface of timidity there lay in me an extremely daring and fearless human being. I had always thought so, but never dared tell anyone. I have often felt as though I had inherited all the defiance and all the passions with which our ancestors defended their Temple and would gladly sacrifice my life for one great moment in history. [1960, p. 202].

Qualities which would one day stand him in good stead, but for the time being, the "daring and fearless human being" had difficulty making ends meet. As Demonstrator at the Brücke Institute he had received a small stipend. Nor was his financial situation improved at the General Hospital, where again he received a pittance. Occasionally he was sent private patients (a practice permitted in Vienna), notably by Breuer, and private pupils, again sent by friends. His poverty was at times overwhelming. When the holes in his coat were too large to allow him to make a respectable appearance, he borrowed a coat from his friend Fleischl, one of Brücke's Assistants. Among other practical gifts, Martha once sent him a tie. "The tie produces for me the hitherto unheard-of luxury of a change of ties, for I still possess another decent one" (1960, p. 91). "I seriously consider having breakfast in my room so as to save money and at the same time eat better food" (1960, p. 99). And always, like a cloud, the poverty of his family hung over him. For a time, while his son was still at the University, Jakob Freud was able to contribute to his support. But as Jakob grew older and his earnings dwindled then vanished, so did the support. "My American [a pupil] is good for only forty florins a month, if he lasts, and altogether won't produce more than 120 florins. Of this sum at least half will have to be put aside for Mother" (1960, p. 147). "I handed over fifty florins to Mother today" (1960, p. 148). Receiving a gift of six bottles of wine from his friend Paneth, he shared them with his family. "Could you imagine me having a thousand gulden in the drawer and letting Rosa and Dolfi go hungry? At least half of it I would give to them . . ." (1960, p. 114). Even far removed from them while studying at the Salpêtrière in Paris and living on his meager traveling grant, concern about his family continued to plague him.

> My new shoes arrived today, with laces and English soles, but twenty-two francs! Altogether, you would hardly believe the amount of money one needs for the most ordinary things, and how poor I am already! Needless to say, I have already written to Paneth [who had suggested that if in need of money, Freud was to write to him]. But my stay here is going to be well worth it, this I can see clearly. If I didn't have to think of the misery at home, I would feel quite all right. But I am so old, and so weak and so wicked that I cannot deny myself a thing. I eat my fill and I smoke and I cannot do anything but—be sorry. Whenever I think of them it upsets me, but this doesn't do them any good. [1960, p. 176]

The necessity to support himself and at the same time to relieve his family left Freud no recourse but to borrow from his friends. The chief donor was Breuer, who supplied him with a monthly sum of money. It is more than likely that the money was meant as a gift. Breuer, however, aware of Freud's pride and vulnerability, may have euphemistically called his gifts loans. These loans were so constant and regular that Fleischl-Marxow, who had private means, protested, feeling himself slighted. Why borrow only from Breuer, and not from him as well? "Within a small and select circle of men who are in accord over the most important things," he instructed Freud, "it would be just as wrong for one of them not to share his opinions with the others as for one of them to be unwilling to accept any help" (Jones 1953, p. 161).

It speaks well for Breuer's delicacy that Freud, for all his sensitivity and pride, was able to continue accepting the monthly sums and to deny, to all appearances, his feeling of indebtedness. "Breuer has urged me to take a great deal of money for the time when he will be away. If it were anybody but him, I would be ashamed, but he proves himself to be such a trusting friend that his money plays a very secondary role" (Freud 1985a, p. 60, fn.). The unnecessary "very" would suggest that the money did not play the secondary role he would have liked, for it seems he *was* ashamed. Jones (1953) cites from another of Freud's unpublished letters: "He [Freud] wrote once, 'Breuer seems to regard these loans as an institution, but I always mind them.' His longing for independence, economic and otherwise, was constant and indeed vehement" (pp. 160–161). Obviously, Freud did not relish the role of receiver, though the giver was his loyal friend Breuer. Exulting in a series of lectures he was giving which temporarily added to his income, Freud enumerated to Martha the blessings the money would bring: Marty and Minna would drink port, his family would be given a regular sum of money every month, he would order a pair of winter trousers for himself, "and if what is left will enable me to relieve Breuer in December, how wonderful! An isolated income of this kind doesn't make much difference to my budget, you know, but should the lectures continue regularly, girl, it will mean the end of the sponger's existence and the beginning of the end of the 'Dalles' [poverty]" (1960, pp. 126–127). So much for Breuer's money playing a "very secondary role."

At the age of thirty, his doubts concerning his future career resolved, Freud set himself up in private practice as a neurologist. Since it was customary for young doctors to begin their practice by seeing a number of patients gratis, Freud's paying patients were at first few and far between, most of them referred by Breuer. "Today my earnings amounted to eight florins, three from a police official and five again through Breuer . . ." (1960, p. 217).

Shortly after opening his office, spurred by an unexpected gift of money Martha had received from a relative, the couple ended their long engagement and were married. Their first child, a girl, was named Mathilde, after Breuer's wife.

Freud reported to Martha's mother and sister: "She [Martha] is the object of the most friendly attention. . . . I can't even remember how often Frau Breuer, Frau Hammerschlag, Paneth *et al.* have called. . . . Each one brings a bouquet of roses. . . . Breuer blows in and out like a comet" (1960, p. 225).

This was in 1887. Eleven years later, in 1898, Freud (1985a) wrote of Breuer to his friend Fliess: "Again and again I am glad to be rid of him" (p. 305). What was it that brought about this violent reversal of feeling in Freud toward the "dearest friend and best loved of men?" What led to the erosion of this warm and long friendship seems primarily to have been a clash of temperaments, the coming face to face, at a critical time, of their private demons. "Breuer once said of himself that he was ridden by the demon 'But' " (Gay 1988, p. 67). Freud's demon was of quite a different order. ". . . a human being's demon," he wrote to Martha, "is the best part of himself, it is himself. One shouldn't embark on anything unless one feels wholehearted about it" (1960, p. 139). Under Freud's surface of timidity, as Breuer had intuitively sensed, there was a "fearless human being," whereas under Breuer's surface of gregariousness lay an inhibiting timidity. Had the two men not collaborated on the publication of their seminal *Studies on Hysteria*, the friendship might have continued and prospered. As early as 1880, long before Freud had even an inkling of where his future interests lay, Breuer had idly told him about the strange case of Bertha Pappenheim, whose hysterical symptoms had miraculously vanished one by one as she recounted, under hypnosis, in what she called "the talking cure," and "chimney sweeping," the psychical traumas that had precipitated their somatic eruption. In the following years Freud treated many an Anna O. and found again and again confirmation of the cause and cure of hysterical symptoms. The logical next step for Freud was to publish Breuer's and his findings. Breuer's reluctance puzzled Freud, until he recalled the closure of the case of Anna O. On his last visit to his patient, after all her symptoms had been removed, Breuer found her in the throes of an hysterical childbirth, which had so shaken him that, after hypnotizing and calming her down, he left the house, never to return. Freud sought to reassure him, recounting a case of his own in which the patient, coming out of her hypnotic state, had affectionately thrown her arms around him. Breuer gave way before Freud's importunities and agreed to publish, though still reluctantly and with the proviso that sexuality be kept in the background. Freud elaborated years later in a letter to Stefan Zweig,

> What really happened with Breuer's patient I was able to guess later on, long after the break in our relations, when I suddenly remembered something Breuer had told me in another context before we had begun to collaborate and which he never repeated. On the evening of the day when all her symptoms had been disposed of, he was summoned to the patient again, found her confused and writhing in abdominal cramps. Asked what was wrong with her, she replied: "Now Dr. B's child is coming!" At this moment he held in his hand the key that would have opened the "doors to the Mothers," but he let it drop. With all his great intellectual gifts there was nothing Faustian in his nature. Seized by conventional horror he took flight and abandoned the patient to a colleague. For months afterwards she struggled to regain her health in a sanitorium. [1960, p. 413]

"I confess that the plunging into sexuality in theory and practice is not to my taste," Breuer wrote to the Swiss psychiatrist, Auguste Forel. (Pollock 1968, p. 723). It was not sexuality as such that Breuer objected to as being a factor in the etiology of hysteria; it was infantile sexuality that was his *bête noire*. Breuer's mother, Bertha, a beautiful young woman like Bertha Pappenheim, had died when her son Josef was three or four years old, at the height of his oedipal phase of development. Bertha Pappenheim's phantom pregnancy may have touched off his own repressed sexual feelings for his mother, precipitating his flight from his patient. "To discover more of psychoanalysis," Pollock (1968) suggests, "would have led to exposure and confrontation of his infantile neurosis and this Breuer could not do. He withdrew from his patient, from other similar clinical situations, from Freud's theories which threatened him, and finally from Freud himself" (p. 724).

But Breuer did not withdraw from Freud himself. It was Freud, unable to endure the rage he felt at what he experienced as Breuer's abandonment, who withdrew from Breuer himself. Convinced and not convinced, pursued by his demon "But," Breuer continued to vacillate. "Recently at the College of Physicians," Freud (1985a) wrote to Fliess, "Breuer gave a big speech in my honor and introduced himself as a *converted* adherent to the sexual etiology. When I thanked him for this in private, he spoiled my pleasure by saying, 'But all the same, I don't believe it.' Do you understand this? I don't" (p. 151). Neither, apparently, did Breuer understand this. Some five years later Breuer sent Freud a patient. "He kept sending the girl back to me whenever I had chased her away in utter despair. Last year I finally began to get on good terms with her, and this year at last I succeeded. . . . She told me that when she confessed her extraordinary improvement to Breuer, he clapped his hands and exclaimed again and again, 'So he is right after all!' " By this time Freud's feelings toward Breuer had undergone so complete a reversal that whatever his old friend might say or do was suspect.

> In this little scene you can recognize the worshiper of success, who professes faith in one of the most popular religions of the world, to which all weak characters adhere. Why did he for years proclaim that I was wrong? It is very nice indeed that one can enjoy oneself twice with each mistake—the first time by having been wrong, which gives one a feeling of superiority, and then by admitting that one has been wrong, which makes one appear noble to oneself and others. [1985a, pp. 413–414]

In "this little scene," as we read it, Freud's rage may have clouded his judgment. It was Breuer, it appears, who had more faith in Freud's skill than had Freud himself, who kept "chasing" the girl away while Breuer kept sending her back. It was Breuer's insistence that led to Freud's ultimate success. Nor did Freud's judgment of Breuer as a physician escape the sweep of his wrath. The man he had preferred above all others to be Martha's family physician became, in the aftermath of the abandonment, lacking in all skill. "Through a lucky card game, not through knowledge or ability, he won the game of life and made his fortune. Woe to him who dares attack him!" (1985a, p. 427).

Added to the pain of the abandonment, Freud felt the weight of his indebtedness to Breuer for the money he had received from him during the lean years of his youth. In 1893, probably before he could afford to, Freud declared his intention of returning the money he had borrowed. It was agreed, however, after an exchange of letters between the two, that the money not be returned at that time. "He [Breuer] ended up behaving so graciously that everything is smoothed over . . ." (1985a, p. 59). Five years later, in a better financial situation, Freud again attempted to repay the loan, sending Breuer a first installment of 500 florins.

> Thereupon a letter arrives for my wife with the return of 350 florins. First, he did not know that the amount had not yet been paid. Second, two years ago, I treated his poor niece B., estimated the cost of the treatment to be 500 florins and accepted only 150 florins. Therefore now the return of the rest with a receipt for 500 florins. Thereupon, of course, in a very polite letter which brags a little about my income, I prove to him that he has nothing to do with the affair B., that the amount in this case is completely different, and so forth. Thereupon he in turn: as long as I had not paid, he had not thought of paying either; but since I had started, he could not lag behind. He would keep the money and send

> me a receipt for 850 florins. All this with the greatest lack of logic, with disdainful condescension and deeply hurt feelings, as well as an unabated need to do good. . . . It is genuine Breuer. It is enough to make one extremely ungrateful for good deeds. [1985a, p. 294]

Freud's anger on this occasion was perhaps not entirely unjustified. Breuer's return of the money revealed an uncharacteristic insensitivity to the feelings of Freud, who was attempting to demonstrate (bragging a little about his income) that now at last he was successful. It may have appeared to Freud that by returning the money, Breuer was implying that to him he was still the impoverished youth unable to make a living. Neither is it unlikely that Breuer was expressing his own resentment; the man whom he had loved and helped in his time of need and to whom he had been a mentor, had now completely forsaken him for a few friend, Fliess.

Many attempts have been made to explain the intensity of Freud's rage toward his former friend. Certainly "incompatible scientific styles," as suggested by Sulloway (1979, pp. 98–99) would not explain so strong an antipathy on Freud's part. Collaborators whose scientific styles are incompatible may amicably choose no longer to collaborate. Kris (1954) points to what he sees as a characterological trait in Breuer which Freud found difficult to live with: Breuer's oscillation between criticism and admiration. First suggesting, as the cause of the breakup of the friendship, Breuer's "pettifogging kind of censoriousness" and his "withdrawing from the fight" when Freud was most in need of a companion, Jones (1953) remains unsatisfied that these were sufficient reasons for the intensity of Freud's rage. "One must conclude that Freud had changed more than Breuer, and the reason for it must have been an internal rather than an external one" (p. 168). The internal reason, Jones suggests, must have been due to some neurotic element, to an unconscious transference from earlier figures in his life, ultimately, his father.

> Breuer was failing in his role as father-protector by repudiating Freud's researches and rejecting his conclusions. Yet how could one with an easy conscience turn against a person who for fifteen years had done so much to help and support one? In early life Freud had found it impossible to hate his father, and had concealed his hostility by love. The same solution was the only feasible one now, but the outer reality forbade it except by the device of "decomposing" the father-person into two, one "good," the other "bad." So hatred was directed against Breuer, and love towards Fliess—both in an excessive degree out of proportion to the merits or demerits of the persons themselves. We know that with Freud intense love and hate were specially apt to go hand in hand. [1953, p. 308]

Jones's idea of decomposing is generally associated with the picture of the very young child who splits the good mother from the bad mother before fusion of the two is achieved. It is therefore more likely that Freud's feelings for Breuer, in their intensity, reached back to his very earliest feelings for his mother. Nor was Freud able to understand the reason for his rage against Breuer any more than he was able, in his self-analysis, to deal with the roots of his idealization of his mother. ". . . no psychoanalyst," Freud declared, "goes further than his own complexes and internal resistances permit . . ." (1910, 11:145). Probing into his unconscious, he was brought up short by a stone wall of resistance which barred the way to exploration of his relationship with his early mother. That Freud felt toward Breuer as a son feels toward his mother is suggested in a curious slip of the pen. Communicating to Fliess the news of the birth of Breuer's grandchild, Freud wrote: "Breuer has become a grandmother . . ." (1985a, p. 66). And when there came at last the parting of the ways, there was nothing the bad Breuer could do to mitigate the rage Freud felt toward the mother surrogate who, in rejecting his researches, had dealt him so severe a narcissistic blow that there could be no recovery, no restitution. Neither could the pain of having been abandoned be assuaged. "I simply can no longer get along with Breuer at all; what I had to take in the way of bad treatment and weakness of judgment . . . finally deadened me, internally, to the loss" (1985a, p. 170). This declaration that he was deadened to the loss is almost immediately contradicted: "I find it very painful that he has so completely removed himself from my life" (1985a, p. 172).

As he was unable to separate from his mother, Freud was unable to separate from Breuer. The bond remained unbroken, in hate and in love. Many years after the dissolution of the relationship, Breuer, by this time an old man, seeing Freud come toward him in the street, opened his arms to him, and Freud, pretending not to see him, walked on (Roazen 1976). On Breuer's death Freud sent his son Robert a letter of condolence, to which Robert replied, telling him that his father had followed the progress of his work with sympathy. To which Freud responded: "What you say about the relation of your father to my later work was new to me and worked like balm on a painful wound that had never closed" (Gay 1988, pp. 481–482).

Freud recounts in his *Psychopathology of Everyday Life* an incident in his own life as an example of unconsciously motivated forgetting, unaware that he is at the same time revealing his inability to deal rationally with his feelings for Breuer. The incident is also recounted in a letter to Fliess:

> I have asked myself why it is that I cannot finish with Breuer, and a recent instance of forgetting provided me with the answer. I had promised Miss L. that I would buy her a small iron strongbox in which she could keep her valuables, but I continually forgot about it. Eventually she reminded me, and I went out shopping for it. I remembered a store, Tanczos, and had the most distinct visual memory of a window in which a small box was to be seen. It must have been someshere in an easy-to-find location in the inner city. But I was absolutely unable to find this place on my walk. So I resolved to look it up in the telephone book or the

> register of business firms before my next walk. But then I forgot about it again on five successive days. Finally I forced myself to remember and looked up the address. And where is the place of this window with the iron box? Brandstratte [Street], across from Breuer, where I must have seen it several thousand times. This is easy to interpret. [1985a, pp. 415–416]

This *is* easy to interpret: Freud was doing his best to avoid and forget Breuer. He tells Fliess, however, that this instance of forgetting provides an answer to the question of why he is unable to finish with Breuer, and we look in vain for the answer. We must attribute this lack of clarity, extraordinary in Freud, to an impregnable resistance to dealing with what he unconsciously defended against knowing: that he could not bring himself to explore the reason for his inability to separate from his mother, symbolized by Breuer.

There can be no doubt that Freud looked back with longing, pain, and rage to the days when he had enjoyed the freedom of Breuer's house, when he could come to Breuer on a hot, exhausting day and be "chased" into the bathtub and then chat with him in his shirtsleeves as the two friends dined together, to the days when he would accompany him on his rounds and be registered as his brother in the *Gasthaus* book of an inn where they spent the night. On Freud's seventieth birthday, Frau Breuer, now a widow, sent him her congratulations. Freud (1960) responded:

> The lines with which you congratulate me on my seventieth birthday have moved me most deeply. The black-edged notepaper reminded me with lightning speed of everything from the moment when, glancing through the door of the consulting room, I first saw you sitting at the table with a barely two-year-old daughter, through all the years when I could almost count myself a member of your family, and the various vicissitudes my life has known since then. Please accept from me in remembrance of this past my most respectful thanks. [pp. 369–370]

The longing and regret Freud felt echoed the feelings of a past beyond remembrance in the furthest reaches of his unconscious.

As for Breuer, it is probable that he instinctively assumed the role of mother in his relationship with his younger friend. Generous and empathic, Breuer's personality had a strong component of what is seen as feminine, or motherly. In his first lecture at Clark University in 1909 Freud emphasized those qualities in Breuer which distinguished him from his medical peers. Whereas other practitioners regarded their hysterical patients as transgressing the laws of science, as heretics in the eyes of the orthodox, and therefore forfeiting the sympathy and interest of the physician, Breuer, on the other hand, though at the time with no more knowledge of the meaning of hysterical manifestations than his fellow practitioners, gave his patient (Anna O.) "both sympathy and understanding, even though, to begin with, he did not know how to help her. . . . Soon, moreover, his benevolent scrutiny showed him the means of bringing her a first installment of help" (1910, 11:11–12).

Breuer's sympathy and benevolent scrutiny—we may well call it motherliness—extended to the destitute whom, like his colleagues and their families, he treated gratis (Ellenbogen 1970). Seventy-three years old at the outbreak of the First World War, Breuer undertook the treatment of wounded soldiers in a distant suburban hospital, commuting there daily despite bad weather or his own fatigue (Pollock 1968). Bolkosky (1982), like Freud, compares Breuer with the more characteristic Viennese doctor of the day. "He was a magical diagnostician and . . . had a phenomenally sympathetic bedside manner. He was therefore unique among Viennese doctors, all of whom were imbued with the Viennese ethic of bureaucratic doctor–patient relationship. . . ." As for Anna O., she "with sympathetic assistance of a physician actually treated herself" and Breuer was "only a passive, permissive, accepting collaborator helping her. Important words: passive, permissive, accepting, helping. They are feminine words of motherliness" (p. 141). And yet, in discussing Breuer as transference figure to Freud, Bolkosky resorts to the stereotypical conception: "Those attributes [of motherliness] Breuer also bestowed on Freud, to whom he was one in a series of father surrogates . . ." (p. 142). But perhaps we should let Breuer have the last word as to how he saw himself in relation to Freud: "Freud's intellect is soaring; I struggle along behind him like a hen behind a hawk" (Freud 1954, p. 13, fn.). Why, of all possible similes, did Breuer choose a hen to designate his relationship with Freud?

In a letter written after the publication of *Studies on Hysteria*, when he and Breuer were drifting apart, Freud foretells the future of his relationship with Fliess:

> I believe he [Breuer] will never forgive that in the *Studies* I dragged him along and involved him in something where he unfailingly knows three candidates for the position of *one* truth and abhors all generalizations, regarding them as presumptions. That everything one enjoys in life has to be paid for so dearly is decidedly not an admirable arrangement. Will the two of us experience the same thing with each other? [1985a, p. 175]

Freud seems to be haunted by the fear that his relationship with Fliess will go the way of his relationship with Breuer. Is there, behind the fear, the wish compulsively to repeat? In his description of what happened between him and Breuer, and in his intimation that the same will happen with him and Fliess, Freud divulges not only the nature of his original relationship with his mother and his ambivalent feelings associated with it, but also his need to reenact this experience with all mother surrogates to come.

4

YOU ARE THE ONLY OTHER

> Our protoplasm has worked its way through the same critical period. How nice it would be if this close harmony between us were a total one.
>
> —Freud

As though to provide a replacement for himself against the time when he would be gone, it was Breuer who brought Freud and Fliess together. In the fall of 1887, the twenty-nine-year-old Wilhelm Fliess, biologist and nose and throat specialist with a flourishing practice in Berlin, came to Vienna for further study. Following the suggestion of an acquaintance, Breuer, he attended the lectures being given by Freud, a man two years his senior. Thus began a friendship which was to last for fifteen years and which, for Freud, was to prove most auspicious.

Slowly making his way into the unconscious after the publication of *Studies*, Freud found himself sorely in need of someone who would help him appraise his discoveries and encourage him to carry on. "At that period," he wrote years later, "I was completely isolated and in the network of problems and accumulation of difficulties I often dreaded losing my bearings and also my confidence" (1914, 14:20). Breuer, as future collaborator or even as sympathetic listener, had failed him. Nor was there another among his peers in Vienna to take his place. "There was no one else," writes Jones (1953), "no one at all, with whom he could discuss the problems that so preoccupied him" (p. 301). Fortunately, in distant Berlin, there was Fliess, a pioneering scientist in his own field, who stood ready to listen, approve, and even make suggestions. Impressed with Fliess's self-confidence and his medical and biological expertise, Freud had set the tone of his future relationship with him in a letter written several months after their first meeting, eight years before the publication of *Studies* and while the sun still shone on his friendship with Breuer. "I still do not know how I managed to rouse your interest; my speculative fragment on the anatomy of the brain cannot have satisfied your severe judgment for long. But I am delighted all the same. So far I have always had the luck to choose my friends among the best of men" (1954, p. 53). Breuer, we note, is still reckoned among the best of men, and Fliess, who had attended his lectures as a student, was a man of such superior judgment that Freud, the lecturer, was fortunate in having roused his interest. And several years later: "When I talked to you, and saw that you thought something of me, I actually started thinking something of myself, and the picture of confident energy which you offered was not without its effect" (1954, p. 60).

As Freud continued to probe deeper into the unconscious and to depend more and more on the encouragement of his distant friend, there flowed a stream of letters, notes, and drafts of manuscripts, from Vienna to Berlin and from Berlin to Vienna. In Freud's salutations in his letters to Fliess we follow the developing intimacy of the relationship over the years, proceeding from Dear Dr. Fliess to Dear Wilhelm, Dear friend, Dearest Wilhelm, My dear Wilhelm, My dear, My beloved friend, Cherished Wilhelm. Separated as he was from his friend by hundreds of miles, the letters became an emotional and intellectual lifeline for Freud. But letters, Freud found, were not enough. "If there are two people," he wrote to Fliess, "one of whom can say what life is, and the other can say (nearly) what mind is, it is only right that they should see and talk to each other more often" (1954, p. 238). And so they did. The two men met, from time to time, at what Freud called a "congress." At these congresses, which usually lasted for several days and which might be held in Vienna, Berlin, or in some city or town carefully chosen for its ambience or to suit their convenience, the two men, freed from professional responsibility, were able to talk and exchange ideas for hours on end. The congresses became a source of invigoration and inspiration for Freud, occasions for which he waited impatiently. ". . . I can barely do without the other—and you are the only other, the *alter*" (1985a, p. 73). "I am in a rather gloomy state, and all I can say is that I am looking forward to our congress as to a slaking of hunger and thirst" (1954, p. 169). "I am diligently making notes of the significant features, to lay before you at the congress. I need you as my audience" (1954, pp. 274–275). "Now look at what happens. Here I live in ill humor and in darkness until you come; I get things off my chest; rekindle my flickering flame at your steadfast one and feel well again; and after your departure, I again have been given eyes to see, and what I see is beautiful and good" (1985a, p. 339).

But Fliess served Freud as more than a mere listening, admiring audience. His impressive erudition in the field of biology, his unfettered flights of imagination, made him a man after Freud's own heart. Since Freud strove mightily to curb in himself a strong inclination toward speculation, he reveled in that of Fliess, serving Fliess as audience just as Fliess, in turn, served him. According to Fliess's innovative theory, which was grounded on the premise of bisexuality in both sexes, all vital activities and processes were determined by laws of periodicity. Jones (1953) succinctly summarizes:

> He [Fliess] thought he had found the key to his periodicity by the use of the numbers 28 and 23; the first was evidently derived from menstruation, the second probably from the interval between the close of one menstrual period and the onset of the next . . . the number 28 referred to the feminine component, 23 to the masculine one; there was the closest connection between them and sexual processes.
>
> These sexual "periods" determined the stages of our growth, the dates of our illnesses, and the date of our death. The mother's periods determined the sex of the infant and the date of its birth. They operated not only in human beings, but throughout the animal kingdom and probably in all organic beings. [p. 290]

Fliess's goal was to establish biology on a firm physical-mathematical foundation, and Freud hoped, in the early years of his research into the etiology of neurosis, to establish, with Fliess's help, a physiological basis for his psychological findings. ". . . perhaps with your help I shall find the solid ground on which I can cease to give psychological explanations and begin to find a physiological foundation!" (1985a, p. 193). As Freud continued with his self-analysis and gained insight into the psychological problems of his patients, the need to find an organic basis for the dynamics of mental functioning lost its relevance. As late as 1898, however, as Freud was drawing close to completing his dream book, Fliess, it seems, still held out the hope of a physiological basis for Freud's work, a basis he himself had been unable to help provide. "I am not at all in disagreement with you," Freud wrote, apparently in answer to a criticism, "not at all inclined to leave the psychology hanging in the air without an organic basis. But apart from this conviction I do not know how to go on, neither theoretically nor therapeutically, and therefore must behave as if only the psychological were under consideration" (1985a, p. 326).

At the outset, the work of the two friends ran parallel. As Freud emphasized psychic determinism in human behavior, Fliess paralleled, in his theory of the laws of periodicity, the determinism of the sexual periods in the processes and vicissitudes of life. "Both men," writes Sulloway (1979), "were strongly united by their common faith in the strict determinism of all vital phenomena, as well as by their desire to achieve a *complete* scientific (i.e., reductionistic) explanation of those vital phenomena that happened to concern their respective medical interests" (p. 138). Fliess's expectation, mirroring his own, could not but be most gratifying to Freud. On one occasion, upon receiving from Fliess notes for what seems to have been a scientific paper, Freud responded:

> My first impression was one of amazement at the existence of someone who was an even greater visionary than I, and that he should be my friend Wilhelm. My conclusion was that I must send the papers back to you, to prevent them from getting lost. In between I found them most illuminating, and said to myself that only a universal specialist such as you could have produced them . . . [1954, p. 130]

Visionary and universal specialist. What more could Freud have desired in one who offered himself as an audience?

So unassailable, it appears, were Fliess's judgments and the correctness of his diagnoses, that those of Freud began more and more to coincide with his.

> I am curious to know whether you will confirm the diagnosis in the cases I sent to you. I am now making this diagnosis very often and agree with you that the nasal reflex is one of the most frequent disturbances. Unfortunately, I am never sure what to do then. The tie to sexuality too is becoming ever tighter; it is a pity we cannot work on the same cases. [1985a, p. 49]

According to another of Fliess's theories, many illnesses—head pain, neurologic pain in various parts of the body, malfunctioning of the organs, of the heart and of the respiratory and reproductive organs—stemmed from a "reflex neurosis" in the nose. All ailments associated with the nasal complex could be relieved by the application of cocaine to the appropriate area in the nose. This theory, too, Freud accepted unquestioningly.

What manner of person was Fliess that he could so enthrall a man of Freud's caliber as to see him as the "new Kepler" of biology, his ill-fated formulations and theories as "earthshaking," and to induce him to so subordinate himself as to derogate his own discoveries? "Perhaps I shall have a few odd things to tell you in return for your great findings and theories" (1954, p. 171). "[I] do not, as you know, think anything of my therapy; and gladly avoid the comparison with your medical activities" (1985a, p. 57). "I once more hold a piece of your scientific material in my hands. So far I have merely glanced at it and fear that respect for so much honest and subtle material will put my theoretical fantasies to shame" (1985a, p. 141). ". . . you altogether ruin my critical faculties and I really believe you in everything" (1985a, p. 56). "I guess I was born to be your claque" (1985a, p. 148). By all accounts, Fliess was richly endowed with self-confidence and charisma. Added to these not inconsiderable attributes were his wealth of biological knowledge, an imaginative grasp of medicine, and a fondness for far-reaching speculation. He also had a "tendency to cling dogmatically to a once-formed opinion" (Kris 1954, p. 4). Eissler (1985) sees Fliess as ". . . evidently an extremely fascinating personality—one of those people who, without being geniuses, give the impression of genius. Whoever met him seemed to fall under his spell" (p. 18). Describing him to his sister-in-law Minna, Freud writes: "He is a most unusual person, good nature personified; and I believe, if it came to it, he would for all his genius, be goodness itself. Therefore, his sunlike clarity, his pluck" (1985a, p. 2). Like

Eissler, Stewart (1967) sees Fliess as a spellbinder and also as incapable of self-criticism, "one who served Freud as an indulgent audience. . . . Yet it is clear that Fliess was a great intellectual stimulant for Freud, probably because Fliess was so unafraid of grandiose formulations" (pp. 20–21).

So it came about that Fliess became for Freud, struggling in isolation with his revolutionary concepts, not just his only audience, his only other, but also, in time, "You shall not refuse me the duties of . . . supreme judge" (1985a, p. 305). A role which Fliess readily accepted. Freud's reliance on Fliess, his utter dependence on his judgment, are best revealed in his references to a dream he had intended for inclusion in his *Interpretation of Dreams* and which he submitted first to Fliess as, presumably, he did with all or most of his writings.

May 18, 1898.

> I shall change whatever you want and gratefully accept contributions. I am so immensely glad that you are giving me the gift of the Other, a critic and reader—and one of your quality at that. I cannot write entirely without an audience, but do not mind writing only for you. [1985a, p. 313]

June 9.

> So the dream is condemned. Now that the sentence has been passed, however, I would like to shed a tear over it and confess that I regret it and that I have no hopes of finding a better one as a substitute. As you know, a beautiful dream and no indiscretion—do not coincide. Let me know at least which topic it was to which you took exception and where you feared an attack by a malicious critic. Whether it was my anxiety, or Martha, or the *Dalles* [poverty], or my being without a fatherland? So that I can omit what you designate in a substitute dream, because I can have dreams like that to order. [1985a, p. 315]

Giving up the dream proved difficult for Freud, for he returned to it again and again.

June 20.

> I have not yet ceased mourning the lost dream. As if in spite, I recently had a substitute dream in which a house constructed of building blocks collapsed ('We had built a *staatliches* house') and which, because of this connection, could not be used. [1985a, p. 317]

October 23.

> The dream [book] is lying still, immutably; I lack the incentive to finish it for publication, and the gap in the psychology as well as the gap left by the [removal of the] thoroughly analyzed sample [dream] are obstacles to bringing it to a conclusion which so far I have not been able to overcome. [1985a, p. 332]

August 1, 1899.

> The loss of the big dream that you eliminated is to be compensated for by the insertion of a small collection of dreams (harmless, absurd dreams; calculations and speeches in dreams; affects in dreams). [1985a, p. 363]

It seems incredible to us today, when Freud's name has become a household word and his concepts a part of our cultural heritage, that he should have so completely subordinated himself to one who, but for his association with Freud, would have long been forgotten. The atmosphere in which Freud worked, however, the climate of the time, makes credible the incredible. Freud's rejection by his peers and his intellectual isolation made Fliess, and his idealization of him, a necessity, and if only an audience of one, at least an audience. Breuer's desertion was more than a severe narcissistic blow; it was an impediment to Freud's progress. ". . . since the scientific contact with Breuer has stopped, I have to rely solely upon myself, which is why progress is so slow" (1985a, p. 86).

Whether Freud could have long continued in complete intellectual isolation is a matter of speculation. "It is questionable," Eissler (1985) believes, "whether Freud, left to himself, would have held out, as in the meantime the situation in Vienna had considerably worsened" (p. 19). And Pontalis (1985), remarking on Freud's idealization of Fliess, asks, pertinently enough: ". . . without that passion, without that still as yet unnamed transference, would psychoanalysis ever have seen the light of day?" (p. xi). The full meaning to him of Fliess's friendship is expressed in a letter Freud wrote on the occasion of the birth of Robert, Fliess's son.[1]

> Your kind should not die out, my dear friend, the rest of us need people like you too much. How much I owe you: solace, understanding, stimulation in my loneliness, meaning to my life that I gained through you, and finally even health that no one could have given back to me.[2] It is primarily through your example that intellectually I gained the strength to trust my judgment, even when I was left alone—though not by you—and, like you, to face with lofty humility all the difficulties that the future may bring. For all that, accept my humble thanks! I know that you do not need me as much as I need you, but I also know that I have a secure place in your affection. [1985a, p. 158]

---

[1]Robert and Fliess's niece, Marianne Kris, both became psychoanalysts.

[2]Following Fliess's injunctions, Freud avoided certain activities during his "critical periods." He may have considered this as contributing to his health. Like Fliess, he suffered from migraine headaches. Concurring with Fliess's theory that the headaches originated in the nose, he applied cocaine, as Fliess prescribed, to the appropriate area in the nose when the headaches occurred. Fliess twice operated on Freud, "probably cauterization of the turbinate bones," according to Jones (1953, p. 309). Like Jones, Schur (1972) believed that what Freud suffered from may have been a chronic nasal infection. At one period in his life, when Freud was suffering severe cardiac symptoms and Fliess, seeing them as exacerbated by nicotine, insisted—in vain, as it turned out—that he abstain from smoking, Freud came to regard Fliess as his trusted physician.

Transference, no doubt, but also with a considerable measure of reality. Discriminating in his choice of friends, Freud could not, no matter how great the need or blurred his judgment, have suffered mediocrity gladly, particularly in one so close as Fliess. Since we do not have the Fliess letters there is no way of gauging, except from references in Freud's letters, the extent of Fliess's contribution to Freud's thinking. In Eissler's view Fliess had a far greater influence on Freud than is generally acknowledged (1971). Gay (1988) sees Fliess's contribution as sponsoring the idea of human bisexuality, which Freud, in turn, elaborated into a cardinal principle. Sulloway (1979) asserts that "along with Brücke, Charcot and Breuer, Wilhelm Fliess is the fourth, the last, and perhaps the most important of the quarternary of personal friends and scientific contemporaries who most influenced Freud's scientific thinking during the crucial years of discovery" (p. 147).

Since the early years of his relationship with Fliess were Freud's crucial years of discovery and since it was Fliess alone to whom he could look for support, Freud's idealization of Fliess was commensurate with his need. Like Breuer before him, Fliess could initially do no wrong. Early in 1895 Fliess came to Vienna at Freud's behest to examine Emma Eckstein, Freud's patient, for any pathology of the turbinate bones and sinuses. Fliess came, operated on Eckstein, failed to remove about a half meter of iodoform gauze with which he had packed the cavity, and returned to Berlin. As a result of Fliess's oversight there followed for Eckstein not only the need for further surgery, but also a series of hemorrhages so severe that "she almost died." As concerned about Fliess's *amour propre* as about Eckstein's critical condition, Freud assured and reassured his friend:

> You did it as well as one can do it. The tearing off of the iodoform gauze remains one of those accidents that happens to the most fortunate and circumspect of surgeons. . . . Of course no one is blaming you. Nor would I know why they

> should . . . rest assured that it was not necessary for me to reaffirm my trust in you once again. [1985a, p. 118]

Clearly, Freud doth protest too much.

Finally, forsaking all reason, Freud submitted to Fliess's suggestion that Eckstein's bleeding had a neurotic base, that is, it was hysterical. When Eckstein at last recovered and was well enough to resume treatment with him, Freud wrote to his friend: "I shall be able to prove to you that you were right, that her episodes of bleeding were hysterical, were occasioned by *longing*, and probably occurred at the sexually relevant times (the woman, out of resistance, has not yet supplied me with the dates)" (1985a, p. 183). Subsequent analysis accommodatingly confirmed Fliess's diagnosis: ". . . so far I know only that she bled out of longing. She has always been a bleeder. . . . When she saw how affected I was by the first hemorrhage . . . she reexperienced this as the realization of an old wish to be loved in her illness, and in spite of the danger during the succeeding hours she felt happy as never before." And it would appear that to entice Freud further after the first hemorrhage, she repeated her seductive hemorrhaging three times in the following days, each time endangering her life, "as an unfailing means of rearousing my affection. . . . She still owes me details and specific dates" (1985a, p. 186). Thus in the end it was Eckstein who was to blame.

It speaks well for the effectiveness of Fliess's self-confidence and charisma that even Breuer, cautious practitioner though he was, called Fliess's gross negligence a "minimal oversight," and Eckstein, Freud reported to his friend, "is a very nice, decent girl who does not hold the affair against either of us and refers to you with great respect" (1985a, p. 123). Schur, however, far removed from the influence of Fliess's personality, wrote of the Eckstein affair: "The previously unpublished correspondence of these months revealed Freud's desperate attempts to deny any realization of the fact that Fliess would have been convicted of malpractice in any court for this nearly fatal error" (cited by Masson in Freud 1985a, p. 121, fn.). As for Freud, his denial and idealization were strained to their limits: "For me you remain the physician, the type of man into whose hands one confidently puts one's life and the life of one's family . . ." (1985a, p. 125).

Like Breuer before him, Fliess served Freud as a mother surrogate at a crucial period in his life, when his need for him was great. Again and again he deplores the distance between them, pleading for greater closeness, for protection against the malevolent forces that threatened. "I . . . hope to be at your place and with you so often that I shall not feel deprived" (1985a, p. 134). "If we lived in the same city—this would have to be Berlin, though, not Vienna—much would have turned out differently and I believe that I never would have gotten into such straits (or would have gotten out of them more quickly). That is why I have so often regretted our separation" (1985a, pp. 307–308). "There has never been a six-month period [following the publication of the dream book, whose reception has "certainly not given me joy"] in which I so constantly and so ardently longed to be living in the same place with you and that which is yours as the one that has just passed" (1985a, p. 405). Separation and deprivation, the burden of Freud's complaints, the greatest fears of the young child, were what Freud most deplored in his relationship with Fliess.

It has been suggested, and by Freud himself, that there was a homosexual component in his relationship with Fliess. "You not only noticed," he wrote to Ferenczi in 1910, when his relationship with Fliess was a thing of the past and when he was warding off Ferenczi's efforts for greater closeness, "but also understood, that I *no longer* have any need to uncover my personality completely, and you correctly traced this back to the traumatic reason for it. Since Fliess's case . . . that need has been extinguished. A part of the homosexual cathexis has been withdrawn and made use of to enlarge my own ego" (Jones 1955, p. 83). Stronger, however, than the homosexual component was the component of the mother–child relationship. Freud seems to have found closeness with Fliess extraordinarily nurturing. "Am I really the same person who was overflowing with ideas and projects as long as you were within reach?" (1985a, p. 123). The feeling of dependency, of deprivation when the loved one is absent, are again the feelings of the young child. The imagery Freud employs in his letters to Fliess is not that of eroticism, but of orality. "I am looking forward to our congress as to a slaking of hunger and thirst" suggests the child in need of sustenance, as, most disconcertingly, does Freud's "hope to receive soon again some crumbs from your table" (1985a, p. 297). Freud postulated that homosexuality was the result of submission to the threatening father. A later theory places the origin of homosexuality, in many instances, in the preoedipal phase of development, flight from the wish to merge with mother. So that, conceding the homosexual component in Freud's relationship with Fliess, it would also seem in accord with the pull toward mother.

At some level, even at the height of his achievement and fame, Freud felt himself to be a deprived child, and his daughters, like his wife, to be mother figures. When his daughter Sophie was about to be married, he sent greetings from Rome to his future son-in-law with "Cordial regards from a wholly orphaned father" (Gay 1988, p. 310). Far more devastating than the loss of Sophie would have been the loss of his youngest daughter Anna, who had, in fact, displaced her mother in the care of her father in his later years. "I too very much miss Daughter-Anna," Freud wrote to Andreas-Salomé in 1922, when he was sixty-six.

> She set off for Berlin and Hamburg. . . . I have long felt sorry for her for still being at home with us old folks . . . but on the other hand, if she were really to go away, I should feel myself as deprived as I do now, and as I should be if I had to give up smoking! . . . therefore in view of all these insoluble conflicts it is good that life comes to an end sometime or other. [Freud and Andreas-Salomé 1972, p. 113]

The only remedy for loss of mother was to die. As for Anna, the feelings induced in her by her father were those of a mother who anticipates with dread the death of her child. "What am I going to do," she wrote to a friend when she was thirty-four, ". . . when I am left alone and thus I lose all that gives meaning to my life? I have always wished that I would then be allowed to die" (P. Heller 1992, p. 116).

Was there something in Freud, perhaps, that induced in others—Martha, Breuer, Fliess, his daughters—a desire to mother and protect? This desire seems to have been induced in Jones as well. "I dimly sensed some slightly feminine aspect in his manner and movements, which was perhaps why I developed something of a helping or even protective attitude towards him . . ." (1955, p. 43).

Jones and Schur, both of whom knew Freud well, find his continuing complaints to Fliess hard to understand. This was not the Freud they knew, a man who bore his pain and suffering with fortitude, even stoicism. "How often have I seen him in agony from the cancer that was eating away his life, and on only one single occasion did a word of complaint escape him. To be precise, it was two words: 'Most uncalled-for' (*höchst überflüssig*)" (Jones 1953, p. 306). Schur, Freud's personal physician for the last eleven years of his life, relates that despite the pain he was suffering, Freud resumed seeing his patients a day or two after most of the surgical procedures he underwent. Pichler, Freud's oral surgeon, came to take for granted his patient's tolerance for pain. One of the procedures, carried out under local anaesthesia, lasted longer than usual. "The anesthetic in all that scar tissue was not working too well. Freud started to moan, and then said simply: '*Ich kann nicht mehr weiter.*' ('I cannot take any more.') Pichler's notes on the procedure report this statement, and end: 'I am curious to know why' " (Schur 1972, p. 414). At the time of his friendship with Fliess, however, Freud had not yet developed this fortitude.

"I have a great talent for complaining," Jones (1953)

quotes Freud as saying (p. 170). In the time of life when mother is seen as all-powerful and capable of the impossible no less than the possible, the discontented child complains to her for her failure to create for him a "rosy existence." Fliess, surrogate omnipotent mother, became the indirect object of Freud's complaints. It has been noted that in his letters to Fliess, Freud is uncharacteristically self-preoccupied. He had, indeed, regressed to the child recounting his tales of woe to his mother, hoping that somehow she would make them vanish. And so he complained in his letters to Fliess, about his loneliness, his rejection by the scientific community, about his health, his poverty, his empty waiting room, the misery of living in Vienna. Noting his habit of complaining and unaware of its source or meaning, Freud seemed puzzled by it. ". . . it must be very distasteful to hear someone complaining all the time. Nor is it the least of my annoyances that I cannot react in any other way" (1985a, p. 328). The compulsion to complain was so deep-rooted that it had become automatic, much to his own puzzlement and annoyance. "All sorts of things displease me in life. . . . It is silly that all these occur to me when at last I once again have an occasion to rejoice" (1985a, p. 337).

Freud could not but sense the unconscious aggression behind his complaints, the implicit demand that mother improve his lot. ". . . for weeks I have been complaining to you whenever I had reason to, risking the danger of alienating you, yet expecting that you would not be alienated . . ." (1985a, p. 384). Why was Freud certain that Fliess would not be alienated? Perhaps because mother is not alienated; she may be annoyed, made to feel inadequate, but whether she likes it or not, she will put up with it. "If ever I should meet you in Rome or Karlsbad, I shall ask you to forgive me for the many complaints I have scattered on the way" (1985a, p. 404). In a letter written by Freud in 1901, toward the end of their friendship, we read: "It is true that it is hard to put up with complainers. This, too, I have come to realize" (1985a, p. 443). Had Fliess, sensing the aggression behind the complaints, finally objected? Or did Freud feel that this may have been one of the reasons for Fliess's withdrawal from the relationship?

For the dependent child it is intolerable that mother be sick. "I am very annoyed, in fact furious, that you two [Fliess and his wife] are not feeling any better. . . . On the whole I do not think it is nice of you to be living in Berlin, when you are missed daily by the likes of us" (1985a, pp. 64–65). "Your headaches leave me hurt and helpless" (1985a, p. 87). "I have no use for headaches on your part in September; I shall be making great demands on you" (1985a, p. 134). Only the child may have headaches. "God keep your head free of migraine for me!" (1985a, p. 147). Reminiscent of "Keep well for your Sigmund." Fully aware that the rational may amicably coexist with the irrational, Freud wrote to Fliess, who had undergone an operation: "It is very unreasonable of me, nor do I understand it fully; I am relating it to you as a phenomenon that evidently I am angry with you because you are doing poorly" (1985a, p. 335).

Deviating from the generally held view of Fliess as a father-figure to Freud, Stolorow and Atwood (1978) see him rather as a mother surrogate, the transference harking back "wishfully to Freud's early ideal period with his mother in which he felt himself to be the sole object of her love and admiration. With Fliess Freud strove to revive that early blissful union of the grandiose self with the idealized maternal object" (p. 230). We would emphasize that it was not union with Fliess that Freud unconsciously strove for, but fusion, with complete loss of boundaries. Freud sought, originally, to achieve this fusion in their scientific work. To begin with, he hoped that his friend would supply him with solid physiological ground on which to base his psychological findings. But this original expectation and hope were to go further.

> My inner joy in suddenly being struck by an idea obviously was related not to the latent proofs but to finding a common ground for the work we share. I hope it will go so far that we

> can jointly build something definitive on it, and thereby blend our contributions to the point where our individual property is no longer recognizable. . . . [1985a, p. 215]

This fusion, were it possible, Freud would have liked for their relationship as well. "Your sleepiness now explains to me my own simultaneous state. Our protoplasm has worked its way through the same critical period. How nice it would be if this close harmony between us were a total one; I would always know how you are and would never expect letters without disappointment" (1985a, p. 301). Though written playfully, the fantasy reveals an unconscious wish. Nor does the playful tone disguise the complaint that Fliess had delayed answering his last letter.

Always suspicious of the so-called accidental and occult, Freud was not averse to seeing, in a coincidence involving him and his friend, a paranormal phenomenon:

> As a consequence of the secret biological sympathy of which you have often spoken, both of us felt the surgeon's knife in our bodies at about the same time, and on precisely the same days moaned and groaned because of the pain, I because of lesser pain—evidently because I could not stand greater pain, as this sample proves to me. . . . In my case it was a large furuncle on the raphe scroti which reminded me of my kinship with you. . . . Since yesterday I am doing well, or walking well, and I have reason to assume that the same kind of change has taken place in you as well. [1985a, pp. 333–334]

We have here not only an example of Freud's readiness to accept the paranormal, but also a misconception and an unfounded assumption, all in the service of unconscious wish fulfillment. As Schur (1972) observes, Fliess's operation and the lancing of Freud's furuncle did not take place at about the same time, but a week apart, and so "Freud had made an error" (p. 160). The error was apparently pointed out to him by

Fliess. "In my inattentive reading," Freud responded to Fliess, "I overlooked your first intimation, that you planned to let yourself in for new experimental tortures" (1985a, p. 333). Schur (1972) attributes the error to Freud's "wish to exculpate himself for his failure to rush to Fliess's bedside for reasons of ambivalence" (p. 160). But this would attribute to Freud a most uncharacteristic evasiveness. We may take Freud's word for it that he had indeed overlooked Fliess's intimation. We understand Freud's "inattentive reading" (in itself most unusual) as having two unconscious motivations: a wish to join his friend in "secret biological sympathy," even in suffering pain, and a need to deny the possibility of danger to the indispensable and loved object in submitting himself to "new experimental tortures." It is also likely that had Freud *not* overlooked the intimation, he might very well have rushed to Fliess's bedside. Also, why had Freud "reason to believe" that Fliess was recovering as quickly as he, since, by his own admission, he was the lesser sufferer, unless it were to satisfy his desire for "biological sympathy"?

For fifteen years, through the publication of *The Interpretation of Dreams*, the friendship continued, with Fliess filling the role of only audience, only other, and supreme judge, and with Freud keeping his ambivalence firmly in check. Then, at a congress held in the summer of 1900 at the Achensee near Innsbruck, which was to be their last, the relationship hit a snag. We learn from Freud's letters that at some time—it is not clear just when—Fliess suggested that Freud was reading his own thoughts into the minds of his patients. ". . . you take sides against me and tell me that the 'reader of thoughts merely reads his own thoughts into other people,' which renders all my efforts valueless" (1985a, p. 447). According to the account given by Fliess five years after the last congress:

> On that occasion Freud showed a violence towards me which was at first unintelligible to me. The reason was that

> in a discussion of Freud's observations of his patients I claimed that periodic processes were unquestionably at work in the psyche, as elsewhere; and maintained in particular that they had an effect on those psychopathic phenomena on the analysis of which Freud was engaged for therapeutic purposes. Hence neither sudden deteriorations nor sudden improvements were to be attributed to the analysis and its influence alone. I supported my view with my own observations. During the rest of the discussion I thought I detected a personal animosity against me on Freud's part which sprang from envy. . . . The result of the situation at Achensee in the summer of 1900 was that I quietly withdraw from Freud and dropped our regular correspondence. [Freud 1954, p. 324, fn.]

That Freud showed a violence does not seem likely. In the most trying circumstances, Freud was not given to violence. He was, on the contrary, remarkable for his restraint and self-control. What seems more likely is that Freud, his *Interpretation of Dreams* behind him, the validity of his theories and the efficacy of his treatment of hysterical patients confirmed many times over, had by this time achieved self-confidence enough to question Fliess's contention that his laws of periodicity "unquestionably" played a part in determining the manifestations of neurosis. It is also likely that Fliess, accustomed to his role of supreme judge, a man with a tendency, in Kris's words, "to cling dogmatically to a once-formed opinion," took umbrage at Freud's temerity in questioning his claim for the laws of periodicity, which, if correct, would undermine all of Freud's dearly-won insights into the etiology of hysteria and the efficacy of psychoanalysis.

In Marie Bonaparte's unpublished notebook, found by Masson in Freud's desk in Maresfield Gardens, she records a discussion she had with Freud on the deterioration of his friendship with Fliess:

> The friendship with Fliess began to decline as early as 1900 . . . when Freud published the book on dreams. Freud

> had not realized this! I taught it to him. His friendship with Fliess made him reluctant to impute envy to Fliess. Fliess could not bear the superiority of his friend. Nor could he tolerate, this time according to Freud, Freud's scientific criticisms . . . [Freud 1985a, p. 3]

According to Freud, then, as reported by Bonaparte, Fliess could not tolerate Freud's scientific criticisms. Could these criticisms, in forceful defense of Freud's discoveries, have been the violence referred to by Fliess? It may well have been at this point that Fliess, stung by Freud's rejection of the laws of periodicity vis-à-vis the manifestations of neurosis, called Freud a mere thought reader.

The friendship limped along for several years after the fateful congress, Freud apparently not realizing at first that Fliess had decided to withdraw, and when becoming aware of it, doing all he could to maintain what had been so precious to him, even offering to co-author a book with him on bisexuality. Fliess, however, kept his distance. The stream of letters back and forth was reduced to a trickle. Finally, on September 19, 1901, all efforts at reconciliation having failed, Freud wrote: "I was sorry to lose my 'only audience'. . . . For whom do I still write?" (1985a, p. 450).

In December of 1928, Freud, now a man of seventy-two, received a letter from Ida Fliess shortly after the death of her husband:[3]

> You perhaps have in your possession letters from Wilhelm addressed to you before your relations became clouded. They probably were not destroyed, although they have lost their meaning to you. If that is the case, would you be good enough and trusting enough, dear professor, to place them

[3]The originals, two letters from Ida Fliess to Freud and two from Freud to Ida Fliess, are in the Jewish National and University Library in Jerusalem. The translations above are in Masson's edition of the Freud letters.

> in my hands? For I am the person who of all people has the deepest interest in them. I want them for no other reason, I assure you. If this is not possible, could you at least lend them to me for a short time? [1985a, p. 5]

Freud responded:

> I hasten to answer your letter, although I cannot at present communicate anything decisive with respect to fulfilling your request. My memory tells me that I destroyed the greater part of our correspondence at some period after 1904. But the possibility remains that a select number of letters were preserved and might turn up after a careful search of the rooms in which I have lived for the past thirty-seven years. I beg you, therefore, to allow me time over Christmas. Whatever I find will be at your disposal, unconditionally. If I do not find anything you will have to assume that nothing escaped the destruction. [1985a, p. 5]

Several days later Freud wrote again:

> I have found nothing so far and am very much inclined to presume that the entire correspondence has been destroyed. But since I have also not found other things that I certainly intended to preserve, for example the Charcot letters, I do not consider the matter closed. Naturally, my promise, should I find something, remains the same. [1985a, p. 6]

In her response, Ida Fliess thanked Freud for having left her "with a glimmer of hope that some day one or more of the letters may be found" (1985a, p. 6).

Like Breuer, Fliess had dealt Freud a most grievous narcissistic blow. Only in destroying Fliess's letters could Freud best express his rage at the abandonment—an analogue of his cutting Breuer dead in the street. "But since I have not found other things that I certainly intended to preserve, for example the Charcot letters, I do not consider the matter closed." Simply put, Freud certainly intended to preserve the Charcot letters, which he valued, in clear distinction to his intention regarding the letters of Fliess. "The late Anna Freud," writes Masson, "in a letter to me, wrote that her father never talked to her about Fliess, except very sparingly toward the end of his life, after his letters to Fliess had been discovered.[4] She judged the reason to be that the breakup was still painful to him, even years afterward" (1985a, p. 4).

Two years before the Freud–Ida Fliess correspondence, in 1926, Freud's seventieth birthday was celebrated by the Vienna B'nai B'rith Lodge, of which he had been a member for many years. In acknowledgment, Freud wrote a letter expressing his gratitude for the friendliness he had always enjoyed as one of its members. His unpopular discoveries having led to the loss of most of his personal relationships, he had found refuge and acceptance in the B'nai B'rith Lodge. ". . . at a time when no one in Europe would listen to me and I had no pupils in Vienna, you offered me your sympathetic attention. You were my first audience" (1960, p. 367).

Had Freud's memory so failed him that he had forgotten his "only audience"? Or, as with Breuer, was he attempting, in whatever way he could, to annihilate the treacherous mother surrogate and so ease the pain of abandonment? But Freud was no more able to separate from Fliess than he had been able to separate from Breuer or from his early mother. Ida Fliess's "faint glimmer of hope" that some day one or more of her husband's letters would be found did not remain merely a

[4]Realizing the importance of Freud's letters, Ida Fliess considered turning them over to the National Library of Prussia. But since Freud's work had been burned in Germany, she thought better of it and sold them to an art dealer, Rheinhold Stahl, on condition that he not offer them to Freud, rightly believing that he would destroy them. Stahl, in turn, sold them to Marie Bonaparte in Paris, who informed Freud of the transaction. Yielding to Bonaparte's eloquent persuasiveness, Freud, who had insisted that she destroy the letters ("I do not want any of them to fall into the hands of so-called posterity.") agreed at last to their preservation.

glimmer. Long after her death, amazingly, in Freud's desk in Maresfield Gardens, Masson found a letter from Fliess which had escaped destruction. And even more amazing, "his [Fliess's] portrait, even after the ending of this great friendship," writes Martin, "remained in father's study in a place of honor" (M. Freud 1958, p. 110). What better demonstrations of the power of the unconscious to undo one's best-laid intentions?

5

MY PREDILECTION FOR THE PREHISTORIC HAS REMAINED THE SAME

. . . everything conscious was subject to a process of wearing away, while what was unconscious was relatively unchangeable . . .

—Freud

When Freud was seventy-five years old, he received from an admirer, Stefan Zweig, a book he had written on a number of famous personalities, *Der Heilung durch den Geist.*[1] One of the studies was on Freud. Commenting on Zweig's treatment of him, Freud (1960) wrote to the author:

> The fellow is actually somewhat more complicated: your description doesn't tally with the fact that I . . . was a passionate smoker (I wish I still were), that I ascribe to the cigar the greatest share of my self-control and tenacity in work, that despite my much vaunted frugality I have sacrificed a great deal for my collection of Greek, Roman and Egyptian

[1]English translation: *Mental Healers*, published in 1933 by Viking Press, New York, and Cassell, London.

> antiquities, have actually read more archaeology than psychology, and that before the war and once after its end I felt compelled to spend every year at least several days or weeks in Rome, and so on. I realize from my experience with art in miniature that this medium compels the artist to simplify, but the result is often a distorted picture. [pp. 402–403]

To Freud, his smoking and collecting of antiquities were so much a part of his personality that to overlook them in a study of him was to present not merely an incomplete, but a distorted picture. In an earlier letter, in answer to a questionnaire regarding his smoking habits, Freud made similar claims for smoking, attributing to it "a great intensification of my capacity to work and a facilitation of my self-control" (Schur 1972, p. 62). Realizing the importance of smoking and the collecting of antiquities to his well-being, Freud called them his "addictions." We understand an addiction as being "rooted in an oral dependence on outer supplies" (Fenichel 1945, p. 377), symbolically, nurturance from mother. Without the daily and immediate nurturance afforded by smoking, Freud claimed that he lacked the capacity to maintain the self-control and the tenacity necessary for his work.

Schur (1972) suggests:

> While the nicotine addiction thus had an important adaptive function in Freud's life, we may speculate that, along with his constant oral frustration during the last 16 years of his life, the addiction may have prevented Freud from penetrating even more deeply into the importance of the "oral phase" for normal and abnormal development. [p. 413, fn.]

In the same vein Schur wrote to Jones in 1955: "Altogether there are many evidences of complicated pre-genital relationships with his mother which perhaps he never fully analyzed" (Gay 1988, p. 505, fn.). It would be illuminating to know what these "many evidences" were that Schur, his personal physician and so close to him during his later years, alluded to. In an unpublished letter to Abraham, Freud admitted that his passion for smoking hindered him in the working out of certain psychological problems (Jones 1955, p. 189). This admission would suggest that Freud may have sensed that his smoking was a link to the pregenital phase of his life. We may say that Freud knew and did not know the source of his addictions. The acting-out implicit in his smoking replaced the exploration necessary for arriving at insight which might have liberated him from his early mother as from his addiction. But this Freud was unwilling, or perhaps unable, to do, preferring the immediate rewards of his addiction. Perhaps his own dread of uncovering his preoedipal conflicts contributed to his resounding reassurance to others harboring the identical dread.

> . . . the final outcome [of psychoanalysis] that is so much dreaded—the destruction of the patient's cultural character by the instincts which have been set free from repression—is totally impossible . . . the work of psychoanalysis puts itself at the orders of precisely the highest and most valuable cultural trends, as a better substitute for the unsuccessful repression. [1910, 11:53]

Apparently, Freud was unable to reassure himself. Nor, perhaps, could be envision a higher and more valuable cultural trend that would serve as substitute for his own repression.

When, occasionally, Freud was forced to abstain from smoking, he was unable to write. During one period of abstinence he informed his friend Arnold Zweig: ". . . I am still alive and as I do not smoke any more I am hardly likely to write anything again—except letters. It reminds me of the Chasan [cantor] of whom it was said: 'he'll live, but he won't sing' " (Freud and Zweig 1970, p. 54). Freud's attempts at abstinence during a period of his friendship with Fliess—when the latter insisted that he abstain from smoking—were doomed to failure, confirming for him time and again his dependence on his cigars for his well-being as for his creativity. ". . . do you really consider it a remarkable boon to live a great many years in misery?" (1985a, p. 63). "I have started smoking again, because I missed it (after fourteen months of abstinence), and because I must treat that mind of mine decently, or the fellow will not work for me. I am demanding a great deal of him. Most of the time the burden is superhuman" (1954, p. 121). If, as he feared, giving up his addiction meant living but giving up his work, Freud chose to sing.

Schur, witness for many years to Freud's moods and habits, confirms his patient's assessment of the importance to him of his cigars. ". . . nicotine stimulated his attention span and secondary process thinking" (1972, p. 412). "It was Freud's contention, based on his own experience, which I could later only confirm, that he needed nicotine during periods of creative writing or the preparation for such activity" (Schur, 1972, p. 61). Schur was naturally greatly distressed by the succession of jaw operations Freud underwent as a result of his addiction. But realizing the importance of nicotine to Freud and its role in his creativity, he came regretfully to accept what he felt he could not remedy.

> I asked myself repeatedly whether I was entitled, or even obliged, to insist more strongly on the enforcement of abstinence. Perhaps a personal physician with the objective detachment of Pichler would have done so. I could not, and in retrospect I realize that I should not regret this fact. It is questionable in any event whether such an attempt would have been successful. [1972, p. 411]

When Freud discovered the suspicious lesion in his mouth, the doctor he consulted, recognizing it for what it was, advised excision, as well as abstinence, "a medically sound but untimely piece of advice," Schur (1972) comments wryly. "Judging from my later experience, this advice [abstinence] was more threatening to Freud than surgery" (p. 350). Surgery, it appears, which symbolizes castration by father, was less threatening to Freud than abstinence, which symbolized separation from mother. "Your question about the cigars," Freud wrote to Eitingon, "induces me to confess that I am smoking again. Considering my age [which was seventy-five] and the amount of discomfort which I have to bear day after day, abstinence and the prospect [of preventing new lesions] which it involves do not seem justified to me" (cited in Schur 1972, p. 412). In other words, the suffering and deprivation he would have to endure were he to give up smoking (separation from mother) would be far greater than the suffering to be endured from new lesions, operations on the jaw, and the clumsy, uncomfortable prosthesis (the "monster," it was dubbed by Freud) he was obliged to wear.

Freud's resistance to exploring his preoedipal past may have been a factor in preventing him, in his clinical work, from exploring the earliest phase of development in his patients. Such exploration might mean activating in himself feelings and fantasies best left repressed. It may be conjectured that, constrained by his inaccessibility to the conflicts of his own earliest years, he judged the conflicts of that period—the narcissistic disorders—to be inaccessible to treatment.

Freud's excessive smoking (the usual quota being twenty cigars a day) could not but have had its effect on his friends and associates. Noting his displeasure when he was the only smoker in the room, most of his colleagues who came to the Wednesday night meetings held in his waiting room became heavy smokers. When they arrived for their weekly meeting, they found all prepared for the hours of presentations and discussions that were to follow, not least the preparations for the smoking—ashtrays, some of them from Freud's precious collection—set on the table before each chair that was to be occupied, and in addition to the refreshments of coffee and cake offered by their thoughtful host, an abundance of cigars and cigarettes. Martin Freud (1958) writes of his visit one night to his father's waiting room after the guests had departed.

> The room was still thick with smoke and it seemed to me a wonder that human beings had been able to live in it for hours, let alone speak in it without choking. I could never understand how father could endure it, let alone enjoy it: which he did. It is possible that to some of his guests the smoke-charged atmosphere was an ordeal, but it is certain they thought the price low to pay for the high privilege of a close personal contact with a great teacher. [p. 110]

Sterba (1982) describes Freud's ceremonious preparation for the inhalation of his most gratifying of nurturances:

> . . . when he sat silently at the meetings listening to the presentations and to the discussions, he often touched an area of his upper jaw as if this gave him some relief from the pain or discomforting pressure. He would then reach for a cigar from the box that stood before him, clip it with a silver cigar clipper that was attached to a long silver handle in the form of a horn, and light it with visible delight. [p. 105]

Generously, and perhaps defensively, Freud was ever ready to share his vice, as he also called his addiction, with those he favored. Offering his seventeen-year-old nephew Harry a cigarette, which was refused, Freud admonished him: "My boy, smoking is one of the most wonderful delights in the world" (1956, p. 313). Schur, a non-relative and perhaps for that reason more in awe of his famous patient, who was forty years his senior, found outright refusal of the offering out of the question.

> When I started my career as Freud's physician he always used to offer me—an inveterate non-smoker—a cigar. Too bashful to refuse, I would puff away at it bravely. Freud

> must have soon noticed this. He once looked at me searchingly and asked with amusement: "Tell me, Schur, are you a cigar smoker?" When I admitted that I was not, he answered: "And you smoke my precious cigars?" [1972, p. 427, fn.]

To one patient, at least, the aroma of Freud's cigars was as the aroma of the burnt offerings to the gods. The poet H. D. (Hilda Doolittle) (1956), who came to Vienna to be analyzed by Freud when he was seventy-seven, describes a session with him:

> He will sit there quietly, like an old owl in a tree. He will say nothing at all or he will lean forward and talk about something that is apparently unrelated to the progression or unfolding of our actual dream-content or thought association. He will shoot out an arm, sometimes somewhat alarmingly, to stress a point. Or he will, always making an "occasion" of it, get up and say, "Ah—now—we must celebrate *this*," and proceed to the elaborate ritual—selecting, lighting—until finally he seats himself again, while from the niche rises the smoke of burnt incense, the smouldering of his mellow, fragrant cigar. [p. 32]

Obviously, we have here a very strong positive transference.

As smoking was the link that united Freud with his archaic mother, the world of antiquities was the happy hunting ground where he went in search of her. Freud called his collecting of antiquities an addiction second only to that of smoking. He chided Zweig for having omitted, from his study of him, the importance of his collecting of antiquities, for which, he claimed, he sacrificed a great deal. And as there was never enough of smoking, there were never enough antiquities to satisfy his craving for the artifacts of the prehistoric past. His first thought, wherever he went, was to visit the museums, and whenever possible, the dealers in antiquities. Surrounded on all sides by the life and din of the present, he went first in search of the buried past. In Paris, where he had gone to study under Charcot, one of his most memorable visits was to the Louvre, the greatest attraction there being the wings housing the antiquities, "the Assyrian and Egyptian rooms, which I must visit again several times . . . a dreamlike world" (1960, pp. 173–174). Arriving in New York on his way to give his lectures at Clark University, the first object of his explorations was the Metropolitan Museum, the chief attraction there being the exhibits from ancient Greece. And when in London, he did not go evenings to the theater, as did other visitors to the city renowned for its theaters since the days of Shakespeare, but spent his evenings reading in preparation for his next day's visits to the museums. Even familiar Vienna did not escape his speculation on what lay under the surface. Lou Andreas-Salomé (Freud and Andreas-Salomé 1972) wrote after an extended visit to the Freuds:

> . . . when we [she and Freud] went out late at night for a walk (often the only time in the day he got out) we talked now and then on quite different matters and he frequently analyzed Vienna, as it were; the streets under the wintry snow reminded him of the city's remotest past. One sensed how easily such a re-creation of the past came to him and one was reminded of the antique objects in his study and that the archaeologist had created the psychoanalyst in him. [p. 230]

We may take Andreas-Salomé's observation a step further and suggest that Freud's creation of psychoanalysis, his compulsion to explore the repressed in man's psyche was, in good measure, a sublimation of his craving for his own repressed past. For Freud, the archaeological process of recovering the forgotten past was replicated in the process of recovering the past in the unconscious. His discussions of his cases are replete with similes and metaphors appropriate to the technique of the archaeologist. "I had no choice," he says of the case of Dora,

> but to follow the example of those discoverers whose good fortune it is to bring to the light of day after their long burial the priceless though mutilated relics of antiquity. I have restored what is missing . . . but like a conscientious archaeologist, I have not omitted to mention in each case where the authentic parts end and where my reconstruction begins. [1901, 7:12]

So inherent in Freud's thinking was the relatedness of archaeology and psychoanalysis that he described his life's work and his hope for its future in archaeological terms: "I was successful in digging up buried monuments from the substrata of the mind. But where I have discovered a few temples, others will discover a continent" (Viereck 1957, pp. 8–9).

Not content with merely viewing the artifacts of the prehistoric in museums, Freud must, whenever possible, acquire and take them home with him. A new acquisition would often be brought with him to the dinner table for several days before being assigned a permanent place in his study or consultation room. There, wherever his glance fell, it would encounter vestiges of the prehistoric past. Whatever Freud earned from single consultations, he put aside for the purchase of his beloved antiquities. ". . . on the next rainy day," he wrote to Fliess from his vacation home in Riemerlehen, "I shall tramp on foot to my beloved Salzburg, where I actually unearthed a few Egyptian antiquities last time. These things put me in a good mood and speak of distant times and countries" (1985a, p. 366). We may take this as a metaphor for his own distant past, the recovery of which would put him in a good mood.

Gedo (1992) sees Freud's *collecting* of antiquities as being driven by

> unconscious emotional needs and could therefore encompass attempts to overcome even his pregenital vicissitudes . . . we might infer that he looked upon his own

> archaic past as his "Egyptian period" . . . the intensity of his need to collect did indeed originate in the preverbal era. In this sense, both the matriarchal aura of Egyptian mythology and the non-alphabetic character of hieroglyphics seem to be especially appropriate to the toddler. [pp. 514–515]

And though every Egyptian artifact might not have a pregenital meaning, and later Roman-Greek artifacts might also have a pregenital meaning, taken as a whole, "it was the Egyptian material that resonated with Freud's earliest psychic experiences" (p. 515).

Once a week, Freud made the rounds of the antiquities dealers in Vienna to see what he could find. And the dealers, on their part, brought him the antiquities they knew he sought when these came into their possession. It was not for their artistic value that Freud amassed his treasures from the past, but to satisfy a never-to-be satisfied need for nurturance. Nor was he concerned with having them on display or arranged in a manner that would set them off to please the eye. More important was their continuous flow into his study and consultation room. Here they occupied every inch of empty space, sometimes, because of their multiplicity, arranged in tiers, and when space was lacking, overflowing onto the floor. Edmund Engelman, a photographer who came to photograph Freud's study and consultation room on the eve of his departure for England, was "overwhelmed by the masses of figurines which overflowed every surface . . . I had been aware of the fact that Freud was a collector of ancient art . . . Nevertheless I was amazed at the unbelievable number of art objects . . . There were only antiquities of great age—Roman, Egyptian, Assyrian, and Etruscan. Wherever one looked, there was a glimpse into the past" (1976, p. 138). One antiquities dealer, Herr Lustig, upon acquiring a mummy case of an Egyptian head dating back to the Twelfth Dynasty, c. 1991–1786 B.C., toted it off to Bergasse 19. Eager to add the artifact to his possessions but feeling he could not afford it, Freud offered Lustig, in exchange for the mummy case, a sum of money and some objects from his own collection. Lustig agreed, and Freud opened a drawer filled with Etruscan mirrors. "Mr. Lustig was so overwhelmed by their numbers he could not even stop to examine them, he said, but 'took the top layer' and departed" (Ransohoff 1976, p. 66).

"My predilection for the prehistoric in all its human forms has remained the same . . ." Freud wrote to Fliess when he was forty-three (1895a, p. 342). And so it remained to the end of his days. Neither time nor illness could diminish Freud's yearning for things past, nor his zest for the pursuit of them. Schur describes Freud's sorrow when traveling was no longer possible for him. "The new excavations in Crete were most exciting events to him and it was deeply frustrating that Fate would not permit him to see its results. He used to show me wistfully any new book that came out about the new excavations" (1972, p. 247). At the age of eighty-two, settled in his new home in London, he wrote to Jeanne Lampl-de Groot that his antiquities, which had been sent on to him from Vienna, had arrived safely, looking more impressive in their more spacious quarters at Maresfield Gardens than they had at Bergasse 19. "There is just one thing," he complained, "a collection to which there are no new additions is really dead" (1985b, p. 313). Since the antiquities, like Freud's smoking, represented feeding, the supply must be constant, lest the child suffer deprivation and die.

A childhood need unsatisfied remains forever unsatisfied, seeking gratification from whatever source available. For Freud, letters, particularly from close friends and associates, were a source of nurturance. And since to receive letters one must write letters, Freud wrote and wrote. It has been estimated that there are between 10,000 and 15,000 extant letters written by Freud. Comparing these figures with those of letters written by other writers of renown, Mahony (1984) submits the following: Lord Chesterfield, approximately 2,600; Horace Walpole, 6,000; Virginia Woolf, 4,000; Voltaire surpassed Freud with 10,000 extant letters out of a total of 20,000; Goethe, whose 14,000 letters take up some fifty volumes. Mahony suggests that the future complete works of Freud would be near 100 volumes, which in large part would consist of his letters, thus making him one of the most prolific letter writers in the history of world literature.

According to his son Ernst (Freud 1960):

> As a letter writer, my father was unusually prolific and conscientious. He dealt with his voluminous correspondence unassisted and in longhand. He answered every letter he received, no matter from whom, and as a rule this answer was in the post within twenty-four hours. His evenings he devoted to scientific writing, but every spare minute between analyses was dedicated to his correspondence. [p. vii]

According to his friend and associate Hanns Sachs, not only were Freud's spare minutes between patients devoted to letter writing.

> All the time I lived near him, I wondered how he managed to accomplish so much. It seemed that the mere mechanic act would take more time than he had spent on writing all these letters, not counting the work of thinking and formulating his thoughts. I asked his family how it was done and they said they did not know either. "He goes to his study and after an hour he brings us ten letters to be mailed" [Sachs 1944b, p. 95]

And the letters must be written in longhand, and by his own hand, Anna only rarely serving as his secretary. "Even in the last weeks before his death when he needed all his strength to hold the pen, the few letters he was still able to write he wrote in longhand" (Sachs 1944b, p. 94). Letters, like his cigars and antiquities being symbolic of nurturance, must be written with his own hand guiding the pen, thus maintaining closeness with mother, and must continue to the end.

Freud's most intimate colleagues, knowing Freud's eagerness for letters, took care to respond as quickly as possible. Eitingon, on one occasion, returning to Berlin after a visit to Vienna, reminded Abraham that he owed Freud a letter. Whereupon Abraham, apologetically and perhaps reproachfully, to Freud: "Eitingon brought me your greetings today. He did not need to remind me that I owed you a letter. I postponed writing to you because I wanted to send you a letter with the Segantini" (Freud and Abraham 1965, p. 96). "Enjoy your leave with your family thoroughly," Freud wrote to Abraham when the latter came home on leave from the army hospital where he had been serving, "but write to me first" (p. 254). Time and again, Abraham, knowing Freud's habit of promptly answering every letter no matter how crowded his schedule or what the condition of his health, pleaded with him to spare himself the trouble of answering letter for letter. "I do not expect a reply to this letter, dear professor" (p. 362). "Your birthday is imminent and as it is not possible for me to bring you good wishes in person this year either, it has once again to be done by letter (and no reply is required)" (p. 381). "If writing is a nuisance for you, dear professor, I shall be content with a few lines from Anna" (p. 389). To which Freud promptly responded: "No, writing is really no burden to me" (p. 390). Not only was it no burden; it was a necessity. Sachs, long settled in America, employed a simple expedient during Freud's last year of life in London to prevent him from responding to his letters; he simply wrote no letters unless he had something important to convey. In Freud's last letter to Sachs (March 12, 1939), he wrote that he was "appalled to find in the heap, amassed on my writing desk, a letter of yours dated February 13th. I don't know if you have guessed for yourself the right explanation of my silence, but feel obliged all the same to confirm your guess and to round it off." The explanation for so serious an offense as not answering a letter from a friend for approximately a month was that Freud had been suffering great pain. "The treatment which was decided on consists in a combination of X-rays from without and radium from within; it is at least a bit more gentle than to cut off my head which would have been the other alternative, and it promises to add some weeks or months of life" (Sachs 1944b, pp. 183–184).

No matter the cost, the flow of letters must continue. The arrival of the postman, bearer of supplies, was the high point of Freud's day, "an event he awaited with great eagerness" (Jones 1955, p. 390). Without letters, as without cigars and antiquities, Freud felt deprived and diminished. On receiving a delayed letter from Jung ("with apologies for the long delay"), Freud replied: "My personality was impoverished by the interruption in our correspondence. Fortunately that has come to an end" (Freud and Jung 1974, p. 76). Fliess, too, had to be reminded of his friend's need for prompt replies. "Remember that I regularly develop the gloomiest expectations when your letters fail to arrive, and write soon to your Sigmund" (1985a, p. 398). Reminiscent of Freud's near panic when a letter from Martha was delayed.

From letters to mushrooms. What better source of supplies than Mother Earth herself? It was not the eating of mushrooms, but the hunt for them that Freud found revivifying. And as with his antiquities, whenever possible he went in search of them. As early as January the Freud family began deliberations on where they would spend their summer holiday and what kind of house would suit them best. One requirement was a good supply of mushrooms in the neighboring forests. And it was Freud, paterfamilias, who set out early in the year to find an appropriate summer house. So keen an eye did he develop for the hiding places of mushrooms that he was able to detect and point them out even when riding in a train (Jones 1955, p. 393).

According to Martin Freud, wise people, knowing that poisonous fungi were often mistaken for mushrooms, the edible fungi, had good reason to refrain from mushroom hunting. But the Freud children were wiser than the wise, for their father had taught them all there was to know about mushrooms. It was he who led his small band of children in the hunt. And there were rules to follow. There was to be no chattering, lest the mushrooms hear them, and the bags they carried must be rolled up under their arms, so that the mushrooms not notice them and take alarm. Martin (1958) writes:

> Father would have done some scouting earlier to find a fruitful area. . . . Once the area had been found, father was ready to lead his small band of troops, each young soldier taking up a position and beginning the skirmish at proper intervals, like a well-trained infantry platoon attacking through a forest. We played that we were chasing some flighty and elusive game; and there was always a competition to decide on the best hunter. Father always won. . . . When father had spotted a really perfect fungi specimen, he would run to it and fling his hat over it before giving a shrill signal on the flat silver whistle he carried in his waistcoat pocket to summon his platoon. We would all rush forward towards the sound of the whistle, and only when the concentration was complete would father remove his hat and allow us to inspect and admire his spoils.[pp. 58–59]

Martin's analogy of the mushroom hunting game organized by his father to the advance of a platoon of soldiers upon the enemy, offers a clue to the meaning of Freud's passion for mushroom hunting. He knew exactly where the quarry was to be found, how to circumvent the risk of being poisoned, how to capture the most desirable of mushroom specimens, how, in short, to wrest from a grudging Mother Earth the gift of sustenance. If mushrooms were not to be found, the favorite quarry was wild strawberries. It was a characteristic of both Freud's favorites that they grew close to the bosom of Mother Earth, and so were a more integral part of her.

Were there perhaps other forms of sustenance Freud might come upon, unexpected supplies in the most unlikely places? "On our long walks on the edge of the sea," Jones

(1955) recounts, "he would stride along swiftly, and I noticed he had to poke every bit of seaweed with his stick, his quick eye darting here and there all the time. I asked him what he expected to find, but got the noncommittal answer 'Something interesting. You never know' " (p. 79).

"His eyes," Sachs observed,

> had the same uncanny quality as his mind . . . namely the ability to see what all others overlooked. This was brought home to me strikingly by a trifle. In the woods of the Tatra [mountains] grew *Herrenpilze*, the most tasty of mushrooms. Freud initiated competitions in hunting them, setting a first prize at a nickel and a second at two cents (20 and 10 Heller) for the most beautiful specimens. But nobody ever touched this money, because he won, every time, both prizes" [1944b, p. 110]

But despite all—the multitude of letters heaped day after day on his desk, the antiquities crowding his study and consultation room, the twenty cigars a day—the feeling of deprivation remained. The postman comes today with his bulging bags of letters, but he must come again tomorrow. He has brought home antiquities from Salzburg, but he will renew his search week after week in Vienna because "a collection to which there are no new additions is really dead." In the early days of his discoveries, Freud feared that recognition would not come in his lifetime. In 1919, when he had a devoted following dedicated to carry on his work, an International Psychoanalytical Association with its branch societies, psychoanalytic journals, and translations of his works in foreign languages, Freud wrote to Abraham: "I think I have finished with sowing but shall not get to the reaping" (Freud and Abraham 1965, p. 299). So famous had he become by the time the Americans entered Austria at the end of the First World War that a member of Wilson's staff came to visit him. And since food was scarce in Austria, "He came accompanied by two baskets of provisions (among them a box of Havana cigars) and exchanged them for copies of the *Lectures* and *Everyday Life*," Freud reported to Abraham (Freud and Abraham 1965, p. 285). What more abundant reaping did Freud desire? Short of complete fusion with mother, it would appear, a state where there would be no conflicts, no strivings to achieve, no desires, drives, frustrations, there was to be, for Freud, no deep-seated satisfaction.

6

I AM WRITING SO MUCH FOR YOU

> A mother is only brought unlimited satisfaction by her relationship to a son; this is altogether the most perfect, the most free from ambivalence of all human relationships. A mother can transfer to her son the ambition which she has been obliged to suppress in herself, and she can expect from him the satisfaction of all that has been left over in her of her masculinity complex.
>
> —Freud

A most puzzling feature of Freud's personality was his seeming distaste for music, all the more puzzling in one of Freud's sensibility who had spent most of his life in Vienna, where music was in the air. ". . . he had not the slightest ear for music," Martin Freud (1958) wrote of his father (p. 37). Freud's nephew, Harry Freud (1956), carries it further: "He despised music and considered it only an intrusion" (p. 313). Jones (1953) recalls Freud's "aversion to music . . . one of his well-known characteristics. One well remembers the pained expression on his face on entering a restaurant or beer garden where there was a band and how quickly his hands would go over his ears to drown the sound" (pp. 17–18). In his own view, Freud had what he called a "stunted acoustic sensibility" (1954, p. 263). But having a stunted acoustic sensibility would not explain the extreme reaction described by Jones. Nor would it explain his banishing the piano from his parents' home, and later, permitting no musical instrument in his own. A stunted acoustic sensibility would suggest, rather, an insensitivity, or indifference, to music.

But Freud's avoidance of music was not absolute. In his student days, according to Jones (1953), Breuer took him to hear *Carmen*, he attended, with Martha, a performance of *Don Giovanni*, an opera he also took his friend Schönberg to hear, and had found *The Magic Flute* rather disappointing. "Some of the arias are wonderfully beautiful, but the whole thing rather drags, without any really individual melodies. The action is very stupid, the libretto quite crazy, and it is simply not to be compared with *Don Giovanni*" (p. 178). Freud's judgment of the "wonderfully beautiful" arias seems incomprehensible for one with a stunted acoustic sensibility. In a letter to Fliess, Freud described his reactions to the *Meistersinger*, which afforded him a "strange pleasure. . . . I was sympathetically moved by the 'morning dream interpretation melody'; I would have liked to add the '*Parnosse*' to 'paradise' and 'Parnassus.' Moreover, as in no other opera, real ideas are set to music, with the tones of feeling attached to it lingering on as one reflects upon them" (1985a, p. 286). Could Freud's enjoyment of music have depended on its being associated with "real ideas"? But this does not seem to jibe with his enjoyment of the "wonderfully beautiful" arias in the "crazy" libretto of *The Magic Flute*. In 1905, in a letter to his family from Rome, Freud gave a humorous description of a performance of *Carmen* he had attended, an opera with which he seemed to be on quite familiar terms. "The great melodies actually come off very well, but everything was a bit coarsened, noisy. . . . Because I like the music which accompanies the card game so much, I stayed on for the third act" (1960, p. 266).

As the years went by, Freud apparently forgot the number of operas he had heard. Kardiner, an American analysand, recalled that "he told me the only opera he had ever heard in his life was *Don Giovanni*" (1957, p. 49). How account for so global a lapse of memory? And why did *Don Giovanni* alone linger in Freud's memory? The figure of Don Juan is popularly seen as a man in constant pursuit of women. A classic analytic view of such a man is that he is uncertain of his masculinity and must therefore seek confirmation of his sexual prowess with one woman after another. In a more recent and perhaps more profound view, Don Juan is seen as unable to establish a lasting relationship with one woman. Such a relationship, symbolic of his relationship with his early mother, would reactivate his original wish to merge with her. Could it have been that Freud's unconscious understood Don Giovanni's unconscious? And if so, did the opera sound so powerful a chord that it reverberated through the years and obliterated the memory of all other operas?

Feder (1991) sees Freud's avoidance of music as having militated against his application of analysis to musical works of art, as he did with other works of art: the novel, drama, painting, sculpture . . .

> . . . only music eluded him. At the Wednesday Night Meetings, Max Graf [father of Little Hans], the musicologist and critic, called for "the unriddling of the secrets of artistic creation" and presented material on musical composition using Beethoven and Wagner as examples. . . . Freud uncharacteristically could not seem to generate much interest in such matters. [p. 18]

Reik (1953), himself a lover of music, ponders the enigma of Freud's avoidance of music. Why, he asks, does music play no role in the work of Freud, which was to the greatest extent based on impressions received by hearing? Reik draws attention to Freud's statement in his *Moses of Michelangelo*, that works of art, particularly those of literature and sculpture, had a strong and lasting effect on him, but it was necessary for him to understand *why* a work of art affected him. "When I cannot do that," Reik quotes Freud, "for instance in music, I am almost incapable of enjoying them. A rationalistic or perhaps an analytic trait in me struggles against my being affected and not knowing why I am so and what it is that affects me." Reik (1953) sees the word "almost" as crucial to an understanding of Freud's avoidance of music:

> The most important part of this statement is the admission that he is or was affected by music. One assumes that he turned away from the emotional impressions of music and that the explanation of his attitude, the pointing to a rationalistic or analytic trait, is a secondary one—we would say, itself a rationalization. It is likely that this turning away, this diversion was the result of an act of will in the interest of self-defense and it was the more energetic and violent, the more the emotional effects of music appeared undesirable to him. He became more and more convinced that he had to keep his reason unclouded and his emotions in abeyance. He developed an increasing reluctance to surrendering to the dark power of music. [pp. 3–4]

But what was it Freud was defending against that made his diversion so energetic and violent? Since it does not seem credible that Freud feared for his reason on hearing music, one must conclude, with Reik, that the reason Freud gave for his avoidance of music, his need to know *why* he is enjoying something, is indeed a rationalization. Freud enjoyed literature, sculpture, mountain climbing, traveling, without first pausing to discover why. Why not music?

Perhaps the key to the enigma lies in his sister Anna's disclosure that her mother was "very musical." How explain, then, that the favorite child of a musical mother had so strong an aversion to music? It is a commonplace that the impressions of early childhood are lasting, the impressions received from mother, the child's first object, particularly so. And no doubt

Amalia, like all mothers, crooned and sang to her son as she held him in her arms, her first-born, bearer of her unfulfilled ambition. Freud's brother Alexander was, in fact, so musical that, according to his nephew Martin (1958), "he could whistle in perfect tune a whole opera" (p. 17). And this without being his mother's favorite. What happened to Sigmund's musicality? It seems likely that his acoustic sensibility was much maligned. Far from being stunted, it was so acute that, in his own words, he struggled against being affected by music, banishing it completely from the house of his parents, and later from his own. Reik's choice of words is suggestive: "He developed an increasing reluctance to surrendering to the dark power of music." It is as though Reik, like Freud, was reluctant to venture further, to identify the dark power which music embodied. To surrender to the dark power was to give up control. What Freud seemed instinctively to fear was the power of music to carry him beyond the boundaries of rationality to those times and places from which, should he reach them, there would be no return. Of all the arts, music, which, it has been claimed, is closest to the Id, is closest to mother.

Wortis (1954), another of Freud's analysands, writes: "Freud suggested that it [the liking for music] was the satisfaction of some deep craving for rhythm . . ." (p. 139). What deeper craving for rhythm can there be but that of being rocked in mother's arms, or even, of being carried in her womb? Sachs (1944a) sees rhythm as going back "to the gaining of pleasure at the mother's breast" (p. 161).

When Freud was eighty years old he wrote to Marie Bonaparte:

> Just received your card from Athens and your manuscript of the Topsy[1] book. I love it; it is so movingly genuine and true. . . . It really explains why one can love an animal like

[1]Bonaparte's chow, about which she wrote a book which Freud and his daughter Anna translated.

> Topsy (or Jo-fi[2]) with such extraordinary intensity: affection without ambivalence, the simplicity of a life free from the almost unbearable conflicts of civilization, the beauty of existence complete in itself; and yet, despite all divergence in the organic development, that feeling of an intimate affinity, of an undisputed solidarity. Often when stroking Jo-fi I have caught myself humming a melody which, unmusical as I am, I can't help recognizing as the aria from *Don Giovanni*:
>
> A bond of friendship
> Unites us both. . . . [1960, p. 434]

Again, Freud's disclaimer to being musical. What he does not disclaim is his intimate affinity with his dog Jo-fi, analogue of the infant whose life he sees as the most ideal of lives: a life of simplicity free from the almost unbearable conflicts of civilization, the beauty of an existence complete in itself. It is significant that Freud hums, when stroking Jo-fi, an aria from his favorite opera in order to establish with his chow, who represents him as an infant, his emotional relationship with his mother during the earliest days of his existence.

Jo-fi died in January 1937, and a month later was replaced by Lün, another chow, related to her predecessor by "a sort of step-relationship." Lün came to England with the Freuds the following year, and to Freud's regret, had to be put in quarantine for six months. Freud's first visit to Lün was reported in *The Referee*, a sporting newspaper.

> Freud found his journey across London tiring. He seemed to find it a great effort even to walk up the path to the front door, supported by his daughter, Dr. Anna Freud. But nothing could have kept the great scientist away from his dog friend. And yesterday I was told by Mr. Kevin F. Quin, head of the quarantine kennels, how Lün leapt to meet him at his approach, glad recognition in every gesture. "It was difficult to say which was more delighted," Mr. Quin told

[2]Freud's chow.

> me. "I have never seen such happiness and understanding in an animal's eyes. [. . .] He played with her, talked to her, using all sorts of little terms of endearment, for fully an hour. And, though the journey is long for a man of his years, he said that he was resolute about coming to see Lün as often as he can." [Molnar 1992, p. 240]

In his preface to *New Introductory Lectures* Freud mentions having had, in earlier years, "the gift of a photographic memory" (1933, 22:5). This gift would seem to be in opposition to a stunted acoustic sensibility. Contrary to his disclaimers, Freud was very much concerned with sound and most sensitive to its emotional and aesthetic effects. When Jones asked him why he spelled the word *Narzissmus* instead of, correctly, *Narzissismus*, Freud replied simply, "I don't like the sound of it" (1955, p. 402).

As surrendering to the dark power of music might lead Freud where he feared but longed to go, a similar danger lurked in yet another area of his life, his love of speculation. From his youth, he felt himself drawn to philosophy, "before I knew what I was intended to do in the world" (1954, p. 141). At the age of sixteen, planning his curriculum for his first year at the university, he wrote to his friend Silberstein that he would "devote all of it to purely humanistic studies, which have nothing to do with my later field but will not be unprofitable for all that. . . . To this end, I shall be attending the philosophy faculty . . ." (1990, p. 24). And a year later, again to Silberstein: ". . . I, the godless medical man and empiricist, am attending two courses in philosophy and reading Feuerbach in Paneth's company" (p. 70). For a time he flirted with the possibility of acquiring two doctorates, a medical degree for practical reasons, and for satisfying his inclination, a degree in philosophy. Many years later, when asked by Jones how much philosophy he had read, Freud replied: "Very little. As a young man I felt a strong attraction towards speculation and ruthlessly checked it" (Jones 1953, p. 29). Why he ruthlessly checked it he did not say, but we assume that he found philosophy not entirely conducive to his peace of mind. Freud put philosophy behind him when he entered Brücke's Institute, where he engaged in non-speculative, scientific research. But far from losing its appeal, speculation remained close to his heart, its indulgence a hope for a later day. "Philosophy," he wrote to Martha, "which I have always pictured as my goal and refuge in my old age, gains every day in attraction . . ." (Jones 1957, p. 41). Though ruthless with himself in checking his inclination for speculation, Freud enjoyed, vicariously, the untrammeled flights of imagination in others, first in his friend Fliess, later in Ferenczi.

> Daring and unrestrained imagination always stirred Freud. It was an integral part of his own nature to which he rarely gave full rein . . . [and which] he displayed to me at times in the hours after midnight when we were relaxing after the time spent in more sedate discussions. It sometimes shocked me slightly, as it doubtless would have Abraham, since we were people always close to realities. [Jones, 1955, pp. 158–159]

"I have an anxious temperament rather than a bold one," Freud wrote to his friend Putnam, "and willingly sacrifice a great deal to have the feeling of being on firm ground" (Jones 1955, p. 182). Apparently, philosophy did not offer the firm ground Freud needed for his feeling of security, though one questions whether the sacrifice to be on firm ground was made willingly, as one questions the anxious temperament in a man who had no qualms about confronting mankind with concepts that challenged their most cherished illusions. These concepts were, however, based on the firm ground of clinical observation. His two great talents, the one for speculation and the other for observation, Freud was able felicitously to combine in the service of his scientific formulations. Nunberg, a member of the Vienna Psychoanalytic Society, describes the process as he observed it in Freud at the meetings of the Society: "What we see first is meticulous scientific observation . . . combined with a soaring fantasy which is restrained by criticism, a need for causality, for systematization and integration" (1962, p. xxii).

The peril to be avoided in pure abstract speculation, we would surmise, was the same peril that lurked in abandoning himself to music: giving up control and so risking the dissolution of his boundaries. Jones suggests that Freud's motive for checking his speculative ruminations was in part the "intellectual perception of the dangers in leading him astray from objectivity . . . there was also the danger of releasing unconscious thoughts for which the time was as yet far from ripe" (1953, p. 34). Could Jones, like Freud, have known and not known?

Often, in periods of stress, as during the First World War or in illness, loss of boundaries might have appeared less fearsome, perhaps even welcome. Then was Freud able, if only in part, to indulge his love of speculation and produce his more speculative works: *Totem and Taboo*, *Beyond the Pleasure Principle*, *Moses and Monotheism*, and the recently discovered *A Phylogenetic Fantasy*, which he wrote in 1915, in the midst of the privations of the war. "In the works of my later years I have given full rein to the inclination, which I have kept down for so long, to speculate" (1925, 20:57). Not quite full rein, since neither were these works products of pure abstract thinking. They were close enough, however, to give Freud a measure of satisfaction.

It was in a discussion with Andreas-Salomé, which she reported in her 1964 *Journal*, that Freud unwittingly revealed the reason for his shying away from abstract thinking.

> He told me a "fantasy" [*Totem and Taboo*] (which he has not yet put down in writing and which I therefore shall not write down either) about the meaning of parricide for the development of civilization from its beginning until now.

> He has never before worked out anything quite so ingenious—almost more ingenious than he usually permits himself to be.
>
> Afterward we spoke about his resistance to pure philosophy. And about his notion that it is really essential to struggle against the need peculiar to thinkers for an ultimate unity in things. . . . Subsequently we talked about the sadness which more and more accompanies our life and experience even when fortune is favorable, about the diminution of our euphoria. . . . Might there not be a connection between the two, the diminished longing for unity and the diminished euphoria? Freud acknowledged that this striving for unity has its ultimate source in narcissism. [1964, p. 104].

Here again we have an example of Freud's knowing and not knowing.

Freud's musicality, not being held in abeyance, like speculation, for refuge in old age, but an exile relegated to the unconscious, surfaced as a derivative of the repressed in his writing and in his speaking. From an early age Freud's writing was remarkable for its beauty of style as for its depth and lucidity. At sixteen, after completing his Matura[3], he reported to his friend Emil Fluss on its results:

> . . . my German paper was stamped with an *exc.* . . . Incidently, my professor told me . . . that I possess . . . a style at once correct and characteristic. I was suitably impressed by this amazing fact and do not hesitate to disseminate the happy event . . . as widely as possible—to you, for instance, who until now have probably remained unaware that you have been exchanging letters with a German stylist. [1960, p. 4]

When, in 1885, Freud applied for the position of lecturer at the University, his chief sponsor, Brücke, submitted a testimonial on his behalf, co-signed by Meynert and Nothnagel, empha-

[3]The examination taken on leaving school.

sizing, among the candidate's attributes, "a gift for elegant literary presentation" (1985b, notes, p. 327). A rare attribute in a doctor submitting scientific papers.

The beauty of Freud's literary style, whether in his writing or lectures, seems to have been instinctive, feeding since childhood on the literature he read and for which his appetite was insatiable. A letter of the still adolescent Freud to his friend Silberstein, though written half defensively, half in jest, contains a clear statement of his self-imposed criteria for the written word. He had had no time to write, he tells his friend, hence his delay in answering Silberstein's letter, for "a letter demands a degree of composure, or artistic calm, a letter is nothing if not an exercise in the so-called liberal arts in which one can take pleasure only when the din of the daily round and cares has been silenced" (1990, p. 64).

When Freud at last completed his momentous *Interpretation of Dreams* and sent it off to the publisher, what was it that nagged away at him? The fear of the furor his revolutionary concepts would rouse? Doubt concerning the scientific validity of his observations? "The dream material is, I believe, unassailable," he wrote to Fliess. "What I dislike about it is the style, which was quite incapable of noble, simple expression and lapsed into facetious circumlocutions straining after metaphors. I know that, but the part of me that knows it and knows how to evaluate it is unfortunately the part that does not produce" (1985a, p. 371). Fliess, apparently, tried to reassure him, but still unsatisfied, Freud wrote again:

> Yet I believe my self-criticism was not wholly unjustified. Somewhere inside me there is a feeling for form, an appreciation of beauty as a kind of perfection, and the tortuous sentences of my dream book, with their parading of indirect phrases and squinting at ideas, deeply offended one of my ideals. [1985a, pp. 373–374]

Referring to the defection of Adler and Jung, Freud (1914) writes: "The truth is that these people have picked out a few cultural overtones from the symphony of life and have once more failed to hear the mighty and primordial melody of the instincts" (14:62). It is not surprising that both the metaphors Freud chose to symbolize his work, the one archaeological and the other musical, are links to the prehistoric period of his life.

Readers of Freud's works in the original see his language as a close second to his scientific creativity, Eissler (1971), in fact, rating it first. "His power to observe, to judge, to draw inferences . . . have to take a secondary place to the genius of his language" (p. 277). To Bettelheim (1983), Freud's language was "the supreme instrument of his craft" (p. 8). In his analysis of Freud's writing, Mahony (1982, 1984) resorts to the vocabulary of musical and literary criticism: fictional mode, orchestration, climactic, movements, momentum, pulsating, polyphonic. . . . Mahony (1984) concludes that Freud was an "artist of Olympian stature and exquisite sensibility" (p. 855).

Following his lecture on hysteria (later published as *The Aetiology of Hysteria*) to the Vienna Society for Psychiatry and Neurology, Freud complained to Fliess that it had been given an icy reception and that Krafft-Ebing, president of the Society, had commented that "it sounds like a scientific fairy tale" (1985a, p. 184). Wolf (1971) poses the question: "Why was this superbly eloquent and beautiful lecture received so icily? Could it be that those sophisticated physicians were offended by sexuality?" Wolf suggests that there may have been a more compelling reason for the icy reception:

> Freud failed to win acceptance not in spite of his beautifully eloquent presentation but precisely because of its aesthetic qualities. When Krafft-Ebing said, "It sounds like a scientific fairy tale" he was telling a half-truth: this work of science did have the beauty of a fairy tale and, to that audience, beauty in a work of science was suspect and unscientific. One can easily imagine that a more pedestrian and awkwardly embarrassed presentation might have been listened to with more respect. Could it be that Freud, a master of empathic understanding,

> did not know this? I would suggest that unconsciously the need to create a work of beauty took precedence over the need to persuade. An artistic work of science became a scientific work of art. [p. 549]

Always his own most severe critic, Freud offers a reason for the fictional quality of his early case histories (*Studies on Hysteria*): ". . . it still strikes me myself as strange that the case histories I write should read like short stories and that, as one might say, they lack the serious stamp of science. I must console myself with the reflection that the nature of the subject is evidently responsible for this, rather than any preference of my own" (Freud and Breuer 1895, 2:160). It was the fault of the material, it would seem, that Freud was an artist.

It is a commentary on the scientific climate of Freud's day that the review of *Studies* by Alfred von Bergner, poet, critic, literary historian, was more accepting than were those reflecting the attitudes of the medical establishment. "We may dimly conceive the idea," von Bergner wrote in his review of *Studies*, "that it may one day become possible to approach the innermost secret of human personality. . . . The theory itself is in fact nothing but the kind of psychology used by poets." And borrowing from Freud's terminology, the reviewer described Lady Macbeth's distress in terms of a "defense neurosis" (Jones 1953, p. 253). For the literary world, Freud's findings gave the stamp of science to their intuitive insights. And for Freud, voracious reader since childhood, the intuitive insights of the creative writer confirmed the insights of psychoanalysis. ". . . creative writers are valuable allies, and their evidence is to be prized highly, for they are apt to know a whole host of things between heaven and earth of which our philosophy has not yet let us dream" (1907, 9:8). Perhaps the poetry of Freud's style as much as the recognition of a fellow traveler in the unconscious was a factor in establishing the kinship. "Poets have always been your allies without knowing it," Hermann Hesse wrote to Freud in 1918, "and they will become more and more conscious of it" (1985b, p. 215). It is no accident that three of the greatest masterpieces in literature, *Oedipus Rex*, *Hamlet*, and *The Brothers Karamazov*, deal with what Freud discovered in the unconscious and named the Oedipus complex.

Jones (1959) describes his first meeting with Freud in 1909, at the first Psychoanalytic Congress. Having read Freud's work, he was familiar with his style of writing, but ill-prepared for the beauty of his spoken word. Freud delivered the first paper of the congress (without notes)—his analysis of "the man with the rats," speaking for three hours, from eight to eleven, when he offered to bring it to a close. "We had all been so enthralled . . . that we begged him to go on." Which he did, for another hour.

> I had never been so oblivious of the passage of time. . . . He spoke as in a conversation, but then his ordinary speech was so distinctive as to be worthy of a literary recording. His ease of expression, his masterly ordering of complex material, his perspicuous lucidity, and his intense earnestness made a lecture by him . . . both an intellectual and an artistic feast. [p. 166]

"Among the things that impressed one about Freud," writes Kardiner (1957), "was his extraordinary facility of speech. . . . Everything he said was practically fit for print; it was incisive, imaginative, filled with metaphors, analogies and stories—particularly Jewish ones—and it was not wordy. Freud talked like a book" (p. 49).

Freud's speaking and writing shared yet another quality which stemmed from his unconscious need for closeness with mother: a reaching out to his audience for intimacy. "The structure of his argument," Riviere (1991) comments with regard both to his writing and his lecturing, "is not built up in a vacuum, as it were; it has a direct reference to the reader; he is addressing you. There is a personal quality, a personal relation implicit in his style" (p. 353). Gay (1976) sees this personal quality as

> empathy raised into a principle of style that led him to take his readers and listeners into his confidence . . . It was this style of empathy that made him cast some of his writings, and not his popularizations alone, in the form of dialogues, and to give his adversaries arguments sound enough to keep the debate interesting and compel him to stretch his power of persuasion to its limits. [p. 31]

The more effectively to render this personal quality, Freud chose to write in Austrian prose, which he considered more flexible than the German.

Seeking closeness with his audience, Freud wrote not for the scientist, but for the educated reader, for "everyman," Ornston (1985) asserts in his paper "Freud's Conception Is Different from Strachey's." Ornston decries a translation which renders Freud's familiar *Ich* into its scientific counterpart: Ego. ". . . Freud's wording is handier and holds up better. There is much more to Freud's ordinary words because they resonate with the ways we all learned to think, and to talk about anything that really matters. Freud sets rhythms and patterns which harmonize with everybody's most intimate experiences and constant bodily intuition . . ." (p. 385). On the same theme, Brandt (1966) writes: "Freud's English translators have rather consistently replaced affect-laden German words by neutral words and dynamic, active constructions by static, passive ones . . . This neutralization and solidification of Freud's central concepts in English has contributed to the tendency to reify them" (p. 50). The most outraged of the protesters against the Strachey translation of Freud's work-seems to be Bettelheim, who believes that "the clumsy substitutions and inexact use of language are all the more damaging to his ideas" (1983, p. 9). Citing as an example of the loss of feeling tone in the English translation of *Mutterleib* (mother's womb) into the more scientific uterus, Bettelheim asks indignantly, "Who would want to return to a uterus?" (1983, p. 52).

Freud himself seemed unconcerned about the quality of the translations of his work. When Jones complained to him about the Brill translation, he shrugged it off, saying that he would rather have a good friend than a good translator.

Faced with an audience in a lecture hall, distracted by the many faces turned toward him, how to achieve the closeness Freud needed for comfort? He would choose one of the many seated before him, and to that one he would address his remarks, imagining, says Reik (1949), "that he was addressing this person alone. And if this person was absent from among his listeners, he would not feel at ease until he had found someone to understudy, so to speak" (pp. 10–11). During one series of lectures, the chosen one was Andreas-Salomé. On one occasion, when she was absent from a lecture, Freud stared unhappily at her empty seat. "I am very sorry," he wrote her, "that I have to answer your letter in writing, i.e., that you were not at my lecture on Saturday. I was thus deprived of my point of fixation and spoke uncertainly" (Freud and Andreas-Salomé 1972, p. 13). Martin Freud's observations concerning his father's attitude toward the telephone underscore Freud's need for closeness with his audience.

> My father hated the telephone and avoided its use whenever possible. As everything in our house was arranged to harmonize with his wishes, all precaution was taken to save him from doing so. . . . My own theory is that when father communicated with another human being, the conversation had to be a very personal thing. [1958, pp. 38–39]

As the beauty of Freud's writing and speaking stemmed from an incorporation of his mother's musicality, so did the need for closeness with his audience stem from his inability to separate from her. Both in writing and in lecturing he communicated with her internalized image. In lecturing, he was impelled to concentrate the idea of an audience into a single person—one felt to be sympathetic—representing the internal image: mother. Speaking on the telephone presented a dilemma. Here he was in communication neither with her internal nor with her external representation. The disembodied voice issuing from the telephone had no analogue in his early childhood experience in which mother's voice and image inseparably merged. Hence Freud's avoidance of the telephone.

Curiously, Freud was able to do his best work only when suffering physical discomfort. "My style has been bad, unfortunately, because physically I have been feeling too well. I have to feel a little unwell to write well" (1954, pp. 295–296). ". . . my head full of dates and ideas about summations, proud of having received some recognition, and with a cocky feeling of independence, I returned to a sense of too much well-being and have since been very lazy because the modicum of misery essential for intensive work will not come back" (1985a, pp. 180–181). Jones observes time and again the relatedness of Freud's creativity to physical discomfort. "He was a chronic sufferer from an obscure abdominal complaint. It was in this part of his person where production seemed to manifest itself to begin with. Increased discomfort, with various other symptoms of general malaise, always preceded Freud's best work" (1955, p. 396).

We are given a most illuminating description of the relatedness of Freud's discomfort to his creativity in one of his letters to Fliess:

> One strenuous night last week, when I was in the stage of painful discomfort in which my brain works best, the barriers suddenly lifted, the veils dropped, and it was possible to see from the details of neurosis all the way to the very conditioning of consciousness. Everything fell into place, the cogs meshed, the thing really seemed to be a machine which in a moment would run of itself. The three systems of neurones, the "free" and "bound" states of quantity, the primary and secondary processes, the main trend and the

> compromise trend of the nervous system, the two biological rules of attention and defense, the indications of quality, reality, and thought, the state of the psycho-sexual group, the sexual determination of repression, and finally the factors determining consciousness as a perceptual function—the whole thing held together, and still does. I can naturally hardly contain myself with delight. [1954, p. 129]

We have in this letter what Wolf might call an example of an artistic work of science or a scientific work of art: the fairy tale opening, the leisurely preparation to heighten the drama of what is about to unfold, the metaphor to concretize the abstract, the rhythmic march of the scientific data mounting in tension until, at last, the coda, the happy ending.

In his paper "Group Psychology" (1921) Freud conceptualized the relationship of mother and son as one based on narcissism. His own involvement with his mother was expressed in part through physical discomfort. This was the stimulus that sent him, by means of his writing, in search of her. When he returned home from a pleasant, carefree vacation with a "cocky feeling of independence," he was not the narcissistic child in need of mother's attention and ministrations. At such times the link that bound him to her, the pain that provided the impetus to create, was missing, and he found himself to be lazy and disinclined to work. "I have always known," Freud wrote to Ferenczi, "that I can't be industrious when I am in good health; on the contrary, I need a degree of discomfort which I want to get rid of" (Jones 1955, p. 346). To be in pain, we would conjecture, sent him in search of mother to heal and comfort. Another factor impelling him to go in search of her via his pain may have been an unconscious feeling of guilt at having abandoned his needy, narcissistic mother who resented his cocky feeling of independence. In his unconscious, Freud may have experienced the pain as a sign of her neglect of him, and perhaps of her anger with him for his laziness and disinclination to work. Only in writing, in creating, would the barriers be lifted, the veils dropped, the boundaries that had separated him from his mother removed, and he would again be her favorite, at one with her and restored through her attentiveness and love. Once restored, however, the link with her was broken, and again he found himself independent, disinclined to work until, the pain returning, he went again in search of her.

Every Sunday morning Freud went to visit his mother, either alone or with several members of his family. And every Sunday morning he developed a stomach ache, an "attack of indigestion," which he attributed to the rich dinner he had eaten at his friend Königstein's house, where he went every Saturday night for his weekly game of tarock (Jones 1955, p. 391). It does not seem likely that Freud would continue to eat a rich dinner every Saturday night that would give him a stomach ache every Sunday morning, unless he felt motivated to have a stomach ache when he went to visit his mother. Roazen (1976) perceptively sees this stomach ache as "a sign of Freud's allowing himself to go back to being a little boy in his mother's presence, an invitation to her tenderness" (p. 46).

Freud was born in a caul, a portent of future greatness, which Amalia did all in her power to bring to fulfillment. She was his spur, his internal audience for whom he wrote and without whom he could not write. "We write in the first place," he wrote to Bonaparte, "for ourselves, following an inner impulse" (Jones 1955, p. 397). "For ourselves" may be read as: for me and my internalized mother, from whom the impulse arises. "The only reason why I write to you so little," Freud wrote to Fliess, his mother surrogate, "is because I am writing so much for you" (1985a, p. 139). Freud's declarations to Fliess: "I need you as my audience," "I cannot write without an audience," were *cris de coeur*, expressions of a desperate need for his friend to listen and be close to him. And when the friendship was over, his bewildered question, "For whom do I write now?" was meant literally. It was inconceivable to Freud that he write for an alien, an unknown, rather than for the demanding mother—or her surrogate—to whom he had been bound since infancy. And when he complained to Fliess again and again about his ailments, this too may be seen as appeals to his mother to remove the pain, since he was writing so much for her.

Sometimes the audience Freud emotionally addressed might be larger, but always his familiars, those closest to him and, as such, mother figures. Hence to Pfister: "I am now writing a paper on Leonardo da Vinci. . . . It will cause plenty of offense, but I write really for a small circle of friends and followers" (Freud and Pfister 1963, p. 34).

The unconscious has its devious ways of asserting its imperatives. Since Freud wrote for his archaic mother, he wrote, not in Latin characters, but more appropriately, in archaic script, whether in his papers or in his letters. But what if the recipient of a letter from Freud was unable to decipher the Gothic script? "Many thanks for your kind letter," Jones wrote Freud at the beginning of their correspondence. "I am ashamed to say it took me two weeks to translate completely, for I am not familiar with old German characters" (Freud and Jones 1993, p. 5). "Since you want me to avoid German characters," Freud responded, "I might as well try to write you in English; you are responsible for my mistakes" (1993, p. 8). But why not German in Latin characters?

> I find it very difficult to write German in Latin script, as I am doing today. All facility—inspiration is reserved for greater matters—deserts me at once. But you have often told me that you cannot read Gothic script, thus leaving me with only two means of communication, both of which interfere with one's intimacy: either to dictate a letter to Anna on the typewriter or to use my clumsy English. [1993, p. 607]

And most revealing of the unconscious motive for Freud's use of Gothic script: ". . . I feel rather weak and incapacitated by influenza (not feverish) and the heightened narcissism of this condition will have been revealed to you in my reverting to Gothic script at the beginning of this letter" (1993, p. 656). Gothic script, then, meant a return to intimacy and closeness with mother, the source of Freud's facility and inspiration.

Freud no doubt sensed the relatedness of his cancerous jaw and his abdominal distress to his mother. He was therefore unwilling to remove or even modify the discomfort and illness which symbolized closeness with the source of his creativity. "Under the influence of analysis [his self-analysis]," he wrote to Fliess, "my cardiac symptoms are now very frequently replaced by gastrointestinal symptoms" (1985a, p. 276). The closer he came, in his self-analysis, to his early history, the more frequently did his symptoms come to symbolize the wish for union with his mother, and were therefore ignored, no matter the cost in pain and suffering. "It is noteworthy," writes Jones (1957), "that he would never renounce smoking on account of his cancerous jaw, nor for his abdominal troubles which seemed also to be affected by smoking, but only for cardiac complications. These he took seriously" (p. 159).

Freud well understood his mother's imperative: I am the mother. He summoned her with the magical gestures of smoking and abdominal pain. With these alone was he able to create. When he was seventy-two he wrote to Bonaparte: ". . . the enormous talent for laziness, which I have always suspected in myself and which had no chance of developing in my fully occupied life, is now coming to expression" (Jones 1957, p. 141). In his declining years Freud felt freer to relax his controls, to engage in speculation, and to enjoy his long-denied prerogative of childhood: laziness. But not entirely. The controls and the habits of a lifetime were too strong to be given up by an effort of will. That mother must be given unlimited satisfaction remained an imperative to the end. When, in 1938, Freud left Vienna to spend his last year in England, he took with him the name and address of an antiquities dealer in north London, and his work in progress, *Moses and Monotheism*.

7

THE JOURNEY IS LONG

Happiness is the belated fulfillment of a prehistoric wish.

—Freud

"I think about the possibility of death every day," Freud told Blanton, his analysand. "It is good practice" (Blanton 1971, p. 48). To his intimates, Freud's thinking about death every day, even when in good health, was as incomprehensible as it was distressing. Jones (1957) reports that even in the early years of their acquaintance "he [Freud] had the disconcerting habit of parting with the words 'Good-bye, you may never see me again' " (p. 279). Nor was Freud's thinking about death a morbid preoccupation. It was what one reflected on with equanimity and if circumstances warranted, with anticipation.

A short time before his seventy-fifth birthday, Freud underwent yet another operation on his jaw. Anna Freud wrote to Andreas-Salomé, telling her the news and informing her that her father would be home by the time she received the letter. Andreas-Salomé responded with a most distraught birthday greeting:

> . . . even if you are home, you will not be free from pain and not without physical discomfort, and this thought is quite intolerable. One would simply like to set to and find a scapegoat on whom one could vent one's wrath. I realize how childish this sounds, but there is a limit to all things. The fact that the immense sum of human love and gratitude which you have evoked in the world cannot conjure up this little scrap of physical comfort which we all so ardently long for you—that is what so utterly shatters me. I simply cannot write a proper birthday letter. . . . [Freud and Andreas-Salomé 1972, p. 192]

Freud, in his response, seemed more concerned about Andreas-Salomé's distress than about his own suffering and decline:

> . . . your letter surprised and disturbed me. I have always found you—I will not say resigned, but at least raised above everything that happened around you and to you, and it seemed to me you were behaving like someone in a violent fury of indignation. Why? Because I have taken a further step on the stony path which leads us out of this existence? But I do not understand; that was after all to be expected, and in some form or other inevitable and will soon be repeated. Indeed the provisional nature of the reprieve and the definitive nature of the final departure were never so clear to me as now. Every expression of regret would run counter to the reminder that I have possessed a large number of those things which men hold dear. [1972, p. 193]

According to Fliess's calculations, derived from his numbers theory, Freud was destined to live fifty-one years. Failing to accommodate this calculation when he reached the age of fifty-one in 1907, Freud made his own calculations: that he would live until February 1918, when he would be sixty-two. To this appointed time—it may be because of the privations he had suffered during the war—he often looked forward with longing and dread. Writing to Ferenczi in 1917, he expressed the satisfaction that the period of waiting would soon be over. "The superstition that my life is due to finish in February 1918 often seems to me quite a friendly idea" (Jones 1955, p. 194). But Ferenczi was unable to share Freud's stoical attitude, and when he expressed his concern Freud reassured his friend: "I hope you will soon be able to convince yourself that it doesn't mean I'm in a bad mood" (Jones 1955, p. 194). The newly appointed date for his departure, February 1918, having come and gone, Freud began to despair, fearing he might be destined to live as long as had his father and his half-brother Emmanuel, both of whom had reached the age of eighty-one, "so there's a gloomy prospect." There were times, even before he was beset with constant physical pain, when, weighing the two in the balance, not being seemed to Freud preferable to being. In response to her greetings on his sixtieth birthday, Freud wrote to Andreas-Salomé: ". . . had I known how little joy I would feel on my sixtieth birthday, my first birthday would probably not have given me pleasure either. Even in the happiest of times it would be but a melancholy event" (Freud and Andreas-Salomé 1972, p. 43). If so, death might even be a cause for celebration, as when one of his favorite authors died. "I celebrated the release [demise] of our dear C. F. Meyer," he wrote to Fliess, "by acquiring the volumes I lacked" (1985a, pp. 335–336). This when Freud was forty-two.

With the advancing years and as his suffering intensified, Freud's friends could look forward less and less to cheering responses to their birthday greetings. On his eightieth birthday, to Arnold Zweig: "With ever less regret do I wait for the curtain to fall for me" (Freud and Zweig 1970, p. 133). Finally, wracked with pain, from his home in England to a poet-friend: "I am now more than eighty-three years old, thus actually overdue, and there is really nothing left for me but to follow your poem's advice: Wait, wait" (1960, p. 460). This time he had not long to wait.

An intriguing aspect of Freud's relationship with his mother was his feeling that she barred the way to his death. "It is frightening when mothers become shaky; they stand between us and our demise" (1985a, p. 358). And on the death of Eitingon's mother, in his letter of condolence: "The loss of a mother must be something very strange, unlike anything else, and must arouse emotions that are hard to grasp. I myself still have a mother, and she bars my way to the longed-for rest, to eternal nothingness" (1960, p. 392). Freud wrote in *The Interpretation of Dreams* that the father's death "was the most important event, the most poignant loss, of a man's life" (1900, 4:xxvi). What of the mother's death? Here was a loss Freud could not bring himself to contemplate, or perhaps whose meaning he was unwilling to grasp.

As Freud waited for the curtain to fall, Amalia, the woman he had once described to Martha as fragile both spiritually and physically, lived on, barring his way to eternal nothingness. And as Amalia lived on, to Freud's longing for death was added a feeling of terror. "It looked for some time," writes Martin, "as if she would live forever, and my father was terrified by the thought that she might survive him and, in consequence, have to be told of his death" (M. Freud 1958, p. 11). Why the terror at the thought of Amalia being told of his death? Freud's concern about his mother may be viewed as an aspect of his narcissistic involvement with her. Death was a return to Mother Earth. Hence the desirability that mother precede him in death and that in due course he reunite with her. For mother to live after his death would mean a drastic separation from her. This thought being too dreadful to contemplate, Freud defended against it by seeing it projectively, as Amalia's distress at *his* death. Also, Freud was well aware of his mother's narcissistic need for him. The more intimate of Freud's student-patients, we recall, paid their respects to Amalia. It is not improbable that this was suggested to them by Freud himself in order, symbolically, to share with her his achievements as well as to soothe and placate her. We may speculate that contributing to the terror at the thought of dying before his mother was fear of her anticipated rage at his leaving her. Such irrational fear must be assigned to early childhood, when the child fears displeasing the omnipotent, punitive parent. Were Amalia to die before him, however, he would be free to live without fear of displeasing her and incurring her wrath and, in good time, which he hoped would be soon, be with her in death as he had been with her in the blissful days of infancy. Subsequently, when Amalia died, Freud showed no sign of grief. In reply to Ferenczi's letter of condolence he wrote:

> Above all my warm thanks for your beautiful words about the death of my mother. It has affected me in a peculiar way, this great event. No pain, no grief, which probably can be explained by the special circumstances—her great age, my pity for her helplessness toward the end; at the same time a feeling of liberation, of release, which I think I also understand. I was not free to die while she was alive, and now I am. . . . [1960, p. 400]

And to Jones, on the same occasion:

> I will not disguise the fact that my reaction to this event has because of special circumstances been a curious one. Assuredly, there is no saying what effects such an experience may produce in deeper layers, but on the surface I can detect only two things: an increase in personal freedom, since it was always a terrifying thought that she might come to hear of my death; and secondly, the satisfaction that at last she has achieved the deliverance for which she earned a right after such a long life. No grief otherwise, such as my ten years younger brother is painfully experiencing. . . . [Jones 1957, p. 152]

For Freud, mother, life, and death were inseparable one from the other. His earliest and probably most deeply rooted convictions were derived from his mother.

> When I was six years old and was given my first lessons by my mother, I was expected to believe that we were all made of earth and must therefore return to earth. This did not suit me and I conveyed doubts of the doctrine. My mother thereupon rubbed the palms of her hands together . . . and showed me the blackish scales of *epidermis* produced by the friction as a proof that we were made of earth. My astonishment at this ocular demonstration knew no bounds and I acquiesced in the belief which I was later to hear expressed in the words: *"Du bist der Natur einen Tod schuldig"* [Thou owest Nature a death]. [1900, 4:205]

It was his mother who introduced Freud both to life and death, death being described as a return to earth. Earth and mother, as she had graphically demonstrated when she rubbed the palms of her hands together, were identical. The woman who had given her child life would reclaim him when she herself returned to Mother Earth. Thus Freud's mother encompassed for him the totality of existence and non-existence.

As Freud and his mother shared a common goal in life, his achievement of greatness, so they shared a common unconscious wish for fusion. This wish is best told in a dream each of them dreamed. In his dream Freud was in a grave: ". . . it was an excavated Etruscan one. . . . The dream seems to have been saying: 'If you must rest in a grave, let it be an Etruscan one. . . .' I woke up in a 'mental fright,' even after the successful emergence of the idea that children may perhaps achieve what their fathers failed to" (1900, 5:454–455). As we would expect, Freud interprets the dream on the oedipal level, the wish fulfillment being the ability to travel to Italy, as his father could not afford to do. What is not clear, however, is Freud's assertion that the emergence of this idea was successful in exposing the underlying repressed material, since the dreamer was not relieved, but was left in a state of mental fright. What did not emerge and what remained to trouble the dreamer was what the ego defended against expressing, even in a dream: the wish to return to his mother's womb (grave = coffin = womb). An interesting feature of the dream is the wit and ingenuity of the unconscious in providing a prehistoric womb for the mother of the man whose predilection was for the prehistoric.

When Amalia was an old woman and her son still her *goldener Sigi* though a man of world renown, she dreamed that she was at his funeral and around the casket were arranged the heads of state of the major European nations (Roazen 1976). Amalia's dream is the counterpart of her son's. You have become famous, the dream says, recognized by the important heads of state. But I, being the mother, am the source of your greatness; you are a part of me, in my womb (casket), and what is yours is mine. As Freud's dream reflects his longing to reunite with his mother, Amalia's dream reflects her longing to reunite with her son. It was obviously Amalia's inability to separate from her son that kept him bound to her, captive of her narcissistic needs.

Like death, Rome was a preoccupation for a good part of Freud's life. In his letter to Stefan Zweig, Freud pointed out that he had failed, in his study of him, to deal with three important aspects of his personality: his smoking, his collecting of antiquities, and that "before the war and once after its end I felt compelled to spend every year at least several days or weeks in Rome. . . ." Why compelled? What is suggestive here is Freud's associative linking of his visits to Rome with his addictions, smoking and the collecting of antiquities, both links to his preoedipal mother. Since long before he could afford to travel, Freud was obsessed with dreams of visiting Rome. ". . . you know my Roman dreams," he wrote to Fliess (1954, p. 279). And indeed how could Fliess help but know, since Freud's letters over the years were peppered with references to these dreams? "You promised me, by the way, a congress on Italian soil, of which I shall remind you in due time" (1985a, p. 262). The reminders continued from year to year, but the due time remained mysteriously elusive. Could it have been Fliess's reluctance? If so, nothing could have prevented Freud from going without him during one of his long summer vacations, or taking with him as a traveling companion, as he often did, his brother Alexander. Whatever the reason for the long delay, Freud continued to express his yearning, but without effect. "And Rome? And Karlsbad? And our long-promised congress on classical soil? I go on putting new layers of resignation over my yearning. I shall be glad to hear from you that one day it will come true" (1985a, p. 387). And while he waited and put new layers of resignation over his yearning, Freud did what he could to bring Rome to himself. "In any case I am not in a state to do anything else, except study the topography of Rome, my longing for which becomes more and more acute" (1954, p. 269). ". . . a fragment of a Pompeiian wall with a centaur and faun transports me to my longed-for Italy" (1954, p. 330).

What was it that kept Freud for so many years, despite his relentless yearning, from visiting Rome? In a letter to Fliess he writes of the "realization of a secret wish which might mature at about the same time as Rome, so, when Rome becomes possible, perhaps I shall throw up the lectureship. But, as I have said, we are not in Rome yet" (1954, p. 280). Jones (1955) surmises that Freud's secret wish was to leave Vienna and settle in Rome. But had Freud seriously wished to settle in Rome he need not have called it a secret wish, since he let it be known on any and all occasions how detestable he found Vienna and how desirable Rome. ". . . I have been back barely three days and all the bad humor of Viennadom has already descended upon me. It is sheer misery to live here and no atmosphere in which the hope of completing something difficult can survive" (1985a, p. 326). An astonishing statement from the man who developed psychoanalysis in Vienna.

"Vienna is Vienna, that is, extremely disgusting" (1985a, p. 409). "I hate Vienna almost personally and, unlike the giant Antaeus, I gather fresh strength as soon as I lift my foot from the hometown soil" (1985a, p. 403).

Why, then, in view of his violent dislike of Vienna, did he not leave Vienna and settle elsewhere, preferably in Rome? Was it fear of being unable to earn a living elsewhere, even after reaching world renown? This does not seem likely. Reik (1971) writes: ". . . he received many honorable offers, and most attractive financially. And yet he always refused. . . . He hated Vienna and loved it at the same time" (p. 85). And his son Martin:

> . . . sometimes my father hated Vienna, and . . . sometimes he loved the old city. He could have left Vienna during the secure years before the Hitler shadow began dimming the city's gay sky; but he never did, nor did he, so far as I know, ever seriously contemplate emigrating. And even at the end, when every consideration compelled him to leave, he left with great reluctance and only after strong persuasion. (1958, p. 48).

This great reluctance, Jones found, was not easy to overcome. The imminent invasion of Austria by the Nazis had failed to stir Freud from his resolve to remain in Vienna. "It undeniably looks like the beginning of the end for me," he wrote to Bonaparte a month before the invasion. "But we have no choice but to hold out here" (Jones 1957, p. 217). There being no choice seems to have been the product of Freud's unwillingness to consider a choice, since even at that late date he turned down all offers of refuge in other countries. Hoping against hope to persuade him, Jones flew to Vienna a day after the invasion.

> The sight on arriving was depressing enough. The airfield was stacked with German military planes and the air was

> full of them assiduously intimidating the Viennese. The streets were full of roaring tanks and also of roaring people with their shouts of "Heil Hitler." . . . As I had feared, he was bent on staying in Vienna . . . he proceeded to argue that he was too weak to travel anywhere; he could not even climb up to a compartment, as one has to with Continental trains. [1957, pp. 218–220]

As his final argument he declared that "He could not leave his native land; it would be like a soldier deserting his post" (1957, p. 220). Freud seems to have seen no discrepancy in being a frail old man of eighty-two too weak to climb to the compartment in a train and a soldier at his post. Tactfully, Jones refrained from pointing this out. Instead, he told Freud the story of an officer who had been blown to the surface by the boiler explosion when the *Titanic* went down. "On being sternly interrogated: 'At which moment did you leave the ship?' he proudly answered: 'I never left the ship, Sir; she left me.' " (1953, p. 294). This story seemed to convince Freud; he was not leaving his country; his country was leaving him. Or symbolically, he was not leaving mother; she was leaving him. Most revealing of Freud's feelings for Vienna were those expressed in a letter he wrote to Eitingon on reaching England: "The feeling of triumph on being liberated is too strongly mixed with sorrow, for in spite of everything I still greatly loved the prison from which I have been released" (1960, p. 446).

Freud's last gesture before leaving for England suggests an ambivalence: did he wish to die in Vienna, or, as he professed in a letter to his son Ernst, in England, which was offering him refuge? Asked by the Nazis before his departure for a certificate declaring that he had been well treated by the authorities, Freud wrote: *"Ich kann die Gestapo jedermann auf das beste empfehlen"* (I highly recommend the Gestapo to everyone), using, Martin points out, "the style of a commercial advertisement" (1958, p. 217). Had the wits of the Gestapo not been dulled by its megalomania, Freud's irony would easily have been perceived, with what consequences it is too painful to contemplate, and Freud may well have died in the prison he greatly loved. "Why . . . at the moment of liberation," Gay (1988) asks, "take such a deadly risk? Was there something at work in Freud making him want to stay, and die, in Vienna?" (p. 628).

Yes and no. According to Freud's nephew, the poet Ernst Waldinger, Freud said gaily when he finally received his immigration papers in May 1938, ". . . Now I'm *Hans im Glück*!" (*Hans in Luck*) (Molnar 1992, p. xxiv). Molnar summarizes the Grimms fairy tale of *Hans im Glück*, Freud's favorite fairy tale, which he often told his grandchildren. Hans has completed his apprenticeship and is paid by his master with a lump of gold as big as his head. Trudging homeward under the hot sun with his lump of gold, which seems to grow heavier and heavier, Hans happily barters it for a horse. The horse grows restive and throws Hans, who then barters it for a pig, which will at least provide him with a delectable meal. But the pig, which proves unmanageable, is in turn bartered for a goose. . . . "And so Hans' journey proceeds through a series of diminishing exchanges until he finally ends up with nothing but two stones, which he accidentally knocks into a well. And then runs home happily to his mother" (Molnar 1992, p. xxiv). It is not difficult to guess why this was Freud's favorite fairy tale.

The receipt of his emigration papers concretized for Freud his identification with Hans. Stripped of all that he had labored for and which constituted his life—his associates long since fled to other lands, his Vienna Psychoanalytical Society disbanded—Freud felt he was going into the world as naked as he had come into it. True, the Nazi authorities had promised to send on his books and antiquities, but could he be certain that the promise would be kept? "Two prospects present themselves in these troubled times," he wrote to his son Ernst before leaving Vienna, "to see you all together once more, and to die in freedom. Sometimes I see myself as a Jacob being taken by his children to Egypt when he was very old. Let us hope that there will not follow an exodus from Egypt. It is time that Ahasver [the wandering Jew] comes to rest somewhere" (M. Freud 1958, p. 218).

England, always a beloved country, now symbolized mother. Like Jacob, Freud was old and his days, he knew, were numbered. His emphasis in his letter to Ernst was not that he was coming to England to live, but to die in freedom. Like Hans, unburdened of all his earthly possessions, he was now free to return to mother, which at this period of his life, meant Mother Earth.

But to go back to Freud's secret wish, which he hoped would come to pass at the same time that he was able to visit Rome. Attached to Vienna as he was, it was not probable that the wish was to settle in Rome, though it might now and then have been a passing fancy. Vienna was home, the city where he had developed a new science, reared a family, won world recognition and acclaim. Vienna was mother, from whom he felt himself unable to separate. The intensity of his expressions of hatred for Vienna may be seen as the measure of the intensity of his love. Led astray by the violence of his expressions of hatred, Andreas-Salomé wrote to him in one of her letters: "I hope all is well with you in the Vienna you like so little and I so much" (Freud and Andreas-Salomé 1972, p. 14). The hostility toward his mother, which he was unable to bring to consciousness, he displaced onto Vienna, an impersonal and safer target for his aggression. Mother-Amalia accepted and loved her son on condition that he achieve, that he be her golden son. And no matter how far-reaching his fame, she would withhold her love if he did not continue to achieve. Vienna, too, was a mother who withheld her love and acceptance. No matter how many and how great his achievements, never could he wrest from her, as he did from the rest of the world, the approval and recognition he so deeply craved. "Another sensitive area," writes Jones (1955), "was the ostracism he had to endure in his own city of Vienna. This he never really got accustomed to" (p. 123). "You will see that my style will improve and my ideas will be more correct if this city provides me with an ample livelihood," he wrote to Fliess (1985a, p. 374). That is to say, symbolically, that if mother nurtures him properly, he will repay her by achieving even more and bringing her even greater glory. The title of professor, virtually a prerequisite for a lucrative practice, was denied him time after time. "In this abundance of visions it leaves me entirely cold that the board of professors has proposed a younger colleague in my specialty for Extraordinarius [associate professor], thus passing me over, if the news is true. It leaves me entirely cold, but it will perhaps hasten my final break with the university" (1985a, p. 228). The fact that Freud found it necessary to repeat that he was left entirely cold by the news that he was passed over would indicate that, on the contrary, the pain was indeed great. Nor would he have considered breaking with the university had the news left him cold.

Even recognition abroad brought Freud no official recognition at home. Sachs (1944b) writes: "At a time when patients came to Freud from all parts of the world, the Viennese among them formed a diminutive minority. Only when international fame became an undeniable fact, Vienna—outside of the academic circles, of course—became impressed" (p. 20). It was from the Bureau of Taxation, after the war, that Freud received official recognition in the form of an expression of doubt as to the accuracy of his declaration of his income, "since it is well known that your fame attracts patients who are able to pay high fees from other countries." To which Freud responded, out of the depth of his pain and frustration, "I note with pleasure this first official recognition which my work has found in Austria" (p. 20).

Freud's love-hate relationship with Vienna was what kept him there. But why did his longing for Rome not bring him, if not to settle, then at least to visit, the city of his dreams? It was not until 1897, when he was forty-one years old, that he could bring himself to visit Italy, and not until 1901 that he finally mobilized himself and entered Rome. What delayed him? The heat of Rome was too great during the summer, he rationalized. But Freud often took short Easter vacations when the heat of Rome would not have been too great.

Aware that in its persistence and intensity his longing for Rome went beyond the normal, Freud (1954) wrote to Fliess: "Incidentally, my longing for Rome is deeply neurotic. It is connected with my schoolboy hero-worship of the Semitic Hannibal, and in fact this year I have no more reached Rome than he did from Lake Trasimene" (p. 236). Freud elaborates in *The Interpretation of Dreams*:

> Hannibal . . . had been the favorite hero of my later school days. Like so many boys of that age, I had sympathized in the Punic Wars not with the Romans but with the Carthaginians. And when in the higher classes I began to understand for the first time what it meant to belong to an alien race, and anti-semitic feelings among the other boys warned me that I must take up a definite position, the figure of the semitic general rose still higher in my esteem. To my youthful mind Hannibal and Rome symbolized the conflict between the tenacity of Jewry and the organization of the Catholic church. And the increasing importance of the effects of the anti-semitic movement upon our emotional life helped me to fix the thoughts and feelings of those early days. Thus the wish to go to Rome had become in my dream-life a cloak and symbol for a number of other passionate wishes. Their realization was to be pursued with all the perseverance and single-mindedness of the Carthaginian, though their fulfillment seemed at the moment just as little favored by destiny as was Hannibal's lifelong wish to enter Rome. [1900, 4:196–197]

Uncharacteristically, Freud's reasoning here fails to persuade. To choose Hannibal as symbol for the "tenacity of Jewry" may perhaps be doing Jewry an injustice, since Hannibal's tenacity did not prevail. To choose Hannibal because, like Jewry, he was Semitic, is again uncharacteristic, since Freud was inclined to celebrate victorious leaders, Semitic or otherwise, rather than losers. It was he who chose the name for his brother Alexander, naming him after Alexander the Great, and named one of his sons Oliver, after Oliver Cromwell. In a dream he had on his way to England in 1938, an exile from his home, he dreamed that he landed at Pevensy, thus identifying with William the Conqueror. The fragile old man who had another year to live was on his way to conquer England. Alexander, Cromwell, William, all, we note, non-Semitic. If a Semitic leader Freud must choose to symbolize Jewry, or himself, why not one of Jewry's own, like Judah Maccabee, whose descendent Freud was professedly proud to be, or David who, a mere shepherd lad with a slingshot, killed the giant Goliath and went on to become king and build an empire? Why Hannibal, who not only did not succeed in entering Rome, but turned back, and when faced with the danger of being handed over to his enemies, committed suicide? When it was found, in 1923, that Freud had developed cancer and it was feared that he might commit suicide, he gave no sign at any time of justifying the fear. In 1938, with the Nazis in Vienna and Freud a virtual prisoner in his home and the prospect for the future not only dim but with the possibility of a violent end, like that suffered by many Viennese Jews, Anna Freud asked her father whether it would not be advisable to commit suicide. He answered indignantly, "Why? Because they would like us to?" (Schur 1972, p. 499). Why, then, did Freud choose Hannibal for his role model? It would appear that the reason was a negative one: like Hannibal, Freud wanted with all his heart to enter Rome, and did not succeed.

Two thousand years earlier than Freud's visits to Italy, Hannibal reached as far as Lake Trasimene, then turned back. In 1897 Freud, too, reached Lake Trasimene, went a bit beyond and caught sight of the Tiber River, then "sadly turned back when I was only fifty miles from Rome" (1900, 4:196). Hannibal turned back from continuing on to Rome because he realized that he could not successfully contend with Rome's superior forces. But why did Freud turn back?

There seems to have been, Freud's biographers agree, "a mysterious inhibition," "a mysterious taboo," which kept Freud from visiting Rome. And somewhere within himself Freud must have been aware of this "mysterious taboo." "Well," he wrote to Fliess, "do you realize that Rome cannot be forced? I frequently have fatalistic convictions of this kind which serve my inertia very well" (1985a, p. 410). Inertia. A strange condition for one who saw himself as a persistent conquistador. Why did the otherwise intrepid Freud not explore the meaning and source of his inertia?

In 1901 Freud suddenly overcame his fatalistic convictions and inertia and entered the city of his dreams. What happened? Freud's biographers are in accord with the explanation that Freud's fear of going to Rome stemmed from his unconscious incestuous yearning for his mother and his childhood Catholic nannie, and that it was only after his self-analysis, which revealed and resolved his oedipal conflicts, that it was possible for him to enter Rome, Mother of Cities, which he equated with his mother and nannie. "What emerges from a consideration of the various associations to the series of dreams about Rome is that his inability to 'conquer' Rome, a forbidden city, was probably based upon his feeling that involved vanquishing his father and possessing his mother, and his fear of the dire consequences" (Grinstein 1980, p. 91).

Freud no doubt shrank from realizing his dream of entering Rome because of an inner prohibition. But perhaps the prohibition Freud felt went deeper than his oedipal desire for his mother, that conflict having been recognized and resolved long before his entrance into Rome. It was in October 1897 that Freud wrote to Fliess of his discovery of the Oedipus complex, "in my case too." But it was not until 1901, four years later, that he was able to overcome his inertia and betake himself to Rome. What Freud had *not* discovered in his self-analysis and what had remained the paralyzing prohibition was his preoedipal involvement with his mother. It is significant that Freud refers to his nannie, who disappeared from his life when he was two years old, as his "prehistoric old nurse" (1900, 4:248). And so, his self-analysis leaving unresolved the source of his prohibition against entering Rome, Freud continued to yearn. Eager traveler though he was, he felt himself growing old, and still unable to mobilize himself to visit Rome. "On the whole I am further away from Rome than at any time since we met, and the freshness of youth is notably declining. The journey is long, the stations at which one can be thrown out are very numerous, and it is still a matter of 'if I can last out' " (1954, p. 310). We would suggest that journey in this case had a reference other than to the geographical, and that length here may be seen as a metaphor for pain or distress. In his discussion of symbolism in dreams, Freud writes: "Dying is replaced in dreams by *departure*, by a *train journey* . . ." (1916, 15:153). To go to Rome meant for Freud dying in the arms of his mother. This, although longed for, was still to be dreaded. Hence the ambivalence. ". . . the stations at which one can be thrown out are very numerous. . . ." We may read this as the expression of a hope that he not be permitted to reach his longed-for goal.

Since his self-analysis had not freed Freud of his prohibition to visit Rome, there must have been some external circumstance so compelling as to sweep aside all fears, inhibitions, and taboos. It was around the turn of the century that Freud's friendship with Fliess came to an end. After the last congress, which the two men held at Achensee in the summer of 1900, the long friendship that had been so nurturing to Freud during the critical years of his intellectual loneliness petered out, Fliess having decided to withdraw and Freud's desperate efforts to sustain it being to no avail. The following year, in September 1901, Freud went to Rome, alone, no need for Fliess or his brother Alexander as a companion. While

Freud had Fliess at his side, Rome remained a distant goal which, though longed for, he was able to resist. But on losing Fliess, surrogate mother, he felt urgently the need to fill the void left by the defection. To go to Rome was to regain the prehistoric mother.

On September 19, 1901, Freud (1985a) wrote to Fliess upon his return from his first visit to Rome:

> I received your card a few hours before my departure. I should write to you about Rome now, but that is difficult. It was overwhelming for me too and, as you know, the fulfillment of a long-cherished wish . . . while I was totally and undisturbedly absorbed in antiquity (I could have worshiped the abased and mutilated remnant of the Temple of Minerva near the forum of Nerva), I found I could not freely enjoy the second [the medieval, Christian] Rome; the atmosphere troubled me. I found it difficult to tolerate the lie concerning man's redemption, which raises its head to high heaven—for I could not cast off the thought of my own misery and all the other misery I know about. I found the third, the Italian, Rome full of promise and likable. [p. 449]

Not contemporary Rome, which he found likable and full of promise, certainly not the second Rome, birthplace of anti-Semitism; it was the prehistoric, pagan Rome, fount of his antiquities, that he longed for and was ready to worship. And here, no doubt, he would have been content to remain, at the breast of his early mother, had it been possible. No matter how numerous his visits to the ancient city, the longing remained, strong and insistent as ever. In 1907 Freud wrote to his family from Rome: "What a pity we can't live here always! These brief visits leave one with an unappeased longing and a feeling of insufficiency all the way round" (1985b, p. 184).

What, then, was the "secret wish" Freud hoped would be realized once he visited Rome? The wish seems to have been, apparently, that having received proper nurturance in Rome, he would gain the self-confidence necessary more aggressively to pursue his goal of attaining a professorship.

> When I came back from Rome, my enjoyment of life and work was somewhat heightened and that of martyrdom somewhat diminished. . . . I could foresee that waiting for recognition might take up a good portion of my life and that in the meantime none of my fellow men would bother about me. And I did want to see Rome again, and take care of my patients, and keep my children in good spirits. So I made up my mind to break with strict virtue and take appropriate steps, as other humans do. [1985a, p. 456]

Breaking with strict virtue and taking appropriate steps meant using pressure and influence to gain his end. Freud turned to Exner, his old teacher, with no results, then to Nothnagel and Krafft-Ebing, asking them to renew their previous proposal for his admission to professorship. When these measures failed, "another force was applied. One of my patients . . . heard of the matter and began to agitate on her own." This most influential patient, who moved in the necessary circles, came to her session one day, beaming and waving an express letter from the minister. So it was accomplished, and Freud was at last awarded his long-denied professorship.

> Public acclaim was immense. Congratulations and flowers already are pouring in, as though the role of sexuality has suddenly been officially recognized by His Majesty, the significance of the dream certified by the Council of Ministers, and the necessity of a psychoanalytic therapy of hysteria carried by a two-thirds majority of Parliament. . . .
>
> If I had taken the few steps three years ago, I would have been appointed three years earlier and been spared all sorts of things. Others are that clever without first having to go to Rome. (Freud 1985a, p. 457)

Freud associates the few steps taken with his having first gone to Rome. For Freud, Rome was and remained an invigorating force. ". . . he instantly recovered his spirits and health" on arriving in Rome (Jones 1955, p. 103). Time after time Rome provided the gusto and energy of youth. "In the incomparable beauty of Rome," Freud wrote to Abraham, "I quickly recovered my spirits and energy, and in the free time between museums, churches and trips to Campagna, finished a foreword to the book on totem and taboo, an expansion of the congress on paper, and the sketch of an article on narcissism, as well as a proof of my propaganda article for *Scienta*" (Freud and Abraham 1965, pp. 147–148). In the fall of 1912, feeling ill and fatigued, Freud canceled a trip to England and went to Rome instead. "I feel strengthened and relieved by the air and the impressions of this divine town," he wrote to Jones. ". . . my forces are coming back and I feel

> *wieder Lust mich in die Welt zu wagen*
> *der Erde Leid, der Erde Glück zu tragen*[1]
> (Jones 1955, p. 95).

We have conjectured that in Freud's unconscious, Rome symbolized the mother with whom he longed to merge. But to merge would mean losing boundaries, losing identity, and so, to die. Hence Freud's dread, his many years of resistance to visiting Rome. Jones writes of an "almost morbid intensity," an "initial anxiety," that Freud felt before embarking on a visit to Rome (1955, p. 395). Once Rome was reached, however, fact and fancy united. Rome was, after all, a city, an early mother only in unconscious fantasy, and Freud, though in thrall to a childhood longing, was yet a man of highly developed faculties, of restraint and self-discipline. Thus the symbolic mother, offering symbolic feeding to her symbolic son, meanwhile energized and revitalized the actual man. Jones gives a description of the energized Freud's visits to Rome:

---

[1]"I feel the urge to face the world again,
To bear life's happiness, to stand its pain."

> There were some special features about Freud's Italian journeys, especially in the earlier ones. . . . One was the restless energy with which he would explore town after town, evidently eager to see in the time all there was. Another was the huge gusto and keen enjoyment of every minute. This contrasted with an initial anxiety before embarking on the expedition, one which at times reached an almost morbid intensity. Apart from the great intrinsic interest of the travels, one must therefore suppose that they represented something even deeper in his mind, something perhaps forbidden which was enjoyed all the more when a preliminary prohibition had become overcome.
>
> I used the word "restless" because of the impression I got from the speed with which Freud covered the ground in his Italian journeys, gutting, as it were, town after town. But in fact it is not at all the right word. It is true that his tempo was fast and that he was extraordinarily untiring, but there was no haste, no hurrying away from one impression in search of others. On the contrary, he would spend hours and hours in one museum or other places of interest, very much concerned with the details of what he was examining. . . . [1955, p. 395]

Jones uses the word "gutting" to describe Freud's visits to the towns of Italy. Another word might be "devouring," or the word Jones uses elsewhere when he writes of Freud's "omnivorous passion for sightseeing" (1955, p. 15). In another context, Jones (1953) writes that "Freud had an extraordinary power of rapid assimilation," and "that week [in Florence] must have given him what it usually takes a month to acquire" (p. 333).

We may say, then, that once the initial dread and inhibition were overcome, Freud symbolically gave himself up to the enjoyment of vigorous nursing at mother's breast. That he experienced his sightseeing as a form of oral gratification is suggested by the imagery in his letters. "I do not know whether I shall be able to afford a trip in September and therefore would very much like to nibble at the splendors of the world at Easter" (1985a, p. 403). "Palermo was an incredible feast, something in which one really shouldn't indulge alone. I solemnly promise that whatever drudgery may be in store for me during the coming year I shall remember that I have already had my share and consumed it . . . But perhaps even more beautiful things are awaiting me in Syracuse" (1960, p. 281). Where, perhaps, an even more incredible feast awaited him.

Freud's mode of travel (Minna, who sometimes accompanied him, said that his ideal was to sleep in a different place every night), his excessive mobility, his relentless search for new objects, new sights to see and assimilate, suggest the hunger and longing he felt when, after recovering from angina of the throat, he was seized with a "gigantic hunger like an animal waking from a winter sleep." Associated with the hunger was the longing he had had for Martha, "a frightful yearning, uncanny, monstrous, ghastly, gigantic. . . ." Freud's hunger for narcissistic supplies—tobacco, antiquities, letters, sightseeing—was insatiable. No matter how much he had seen and assimilated in Italy, he came away with an "unappeased longing and a feeling of insufficiency." Hence, in his letter to Eduardo Weiss when he could no longer travel, his expression of grief: "One of the consequences of my failing health difficult to bear is that I can no longer come to Rome" (1960, p. 416).

Before leaving Vienna for England, Freud wrote to his son Ernst that it was time "that Ahasver comes to rest somewhere." But was Freud in truth a wanderer? A resident of Vienna for seventy-eight years, the only possible reason Freud could have had for seeing himself as a wanderer was his perpetual quest for his early mother, by way of his smoking, his acquisitions, his passionate sightseeing wherever he went. "For selfish reasons," he wrote Jung when he was sixty-three, "I want very much to take—without interruption—the trip to my beloved Mediterranean world" (Freud and Jung 1974, p. 278). The trip, we note, is to the cradle of civilization. "Something in me rebels," he wrote to Ferenczi,

> against the compulsion to go on earning money which is never enough, and to continue with the same psychological devices that for thirty years have kept me upright in the face of my contempt of people and the detestable world. Strange secret yearnings rise in me—perhaps from my ancestral heritage—for the East and the Mediterranean and for a life of quite another kind: wishes from late childhood never to be fulfilled. . . . [Jones 1957, pp. 83–84]

The examples Freud gives of what he is rebelling against are the ambitions and strivings of the oedipal child who wishes to compete with his father. What he longs for, in these words to Ferenczi, however, are rather the wishes of the younger child to nurse and absorb. But why refer to these yearnings as strange and secret? Since the oedipal feelings, thanks to his discoveries, could no longer be regarded as either strange or secret, these adjectives must apply to the preoedipal feelings Freud had not identified but sensed to be strange, and must therefore be kept secret.

Freud wrote that "happiness is the belated fulfillment of a prehistoric wish" (1985a, p. 294). In 1939, when he was eighty-three, Freud's prehistoric wish was fulfilled. And though his ashes were not consigned to an Etruscan grave, they were placed, before burial, in a Grecian urn which had been presented to him by Marie Bonaparte on his seventieth birthday and of which he had said, "It is a pity one cannot take it into the grave." Thus were two of Freud's wishes fulfilled.

POSTSCRIPT

"Our complexes," Freud observed to an interviewer, "are the sources of our weakness; they are also often the source of our strength" (Viereck 1957, p. 6). This may explain in part the phenomenon that, though narcissistically bound to his mother, Freud was able to rise to the very heights of creativity. Had his mother been Frau Fluss and not Amalia, would he have been driven to achieve, to overcome, to create psychoanalysis? Out of his feeling of deprivation, too, a graciousness, an empathy, a concern for others, were born. Dependence on his primary provider, a continuing undercurrent of his emotional life, transformed him, reactively, into the provider. The impoverished student who was obliged to borrow from his friends, not only craved independence, but desired with all his heart to reverse the role and become the giver. As a lad of sixteen he said to his six-year-old brother, "Look Alexander, our family is like a book. You and I are the first and the last of the children, so we are like the strong covers that have to support and protect the weak sisters who were born after me and before you" (A. Freud 1985, p. 59).

"Giving presents was one of Freud's great delights," writes Jones (1955). "So much so that he was too impatient to wait for the appropriate moment. Despite his wife's protests, a birthday present to a child always reached its destination on the evening before" (p. 390). "Rare is the guest," Viereck wrote after an interview with Freud, "who leaves his presence without some gift, some token of hospitality!" (1957, p. 11). Viereck had no doubt received after the interview a token of his host's hospitality. After his first visit to Freud, Abraham found in his briefcase, when he returned with it to his hotel, a box containing two Egyptian figurines from Freud's collection, and after another visit, was told that Freud had preceded him to the hotel and paid his bill.

Eissler views Freud's giving and receiving as an expression of his life's balance. "We know for sure that Freud derived an exquisite pleasure from the giving of gifts. When he wrote to his lifelong friend Rie: 'To many I have been, apart from you, permitted to give something; from you fate has let me only take' I believe he correctly described his life's balance between giving and receiving" (1971, pp. 10–11). But perhaps Freud preferred that the scales be tipped more heavily on the side of giving.

Unconsciously identifying with the child who longed to receive, and defending against this need with as strong a longing to give, the business of giving gifts presented a dilemma. How be the one without at the same time being the other? This dilemma Freud formulated neatly in a letter to Frau Abraham after presenting her husband with a sum of money to buy gifts for his two small children—bicycles, as it turned out. The Abraham children, like all well-bred children, sent Freud thank-you letters, and Freud responded, not to them but to their mother. ". . . I should have answered them myself, but I was afraid of undermining their morale, because I should have had to confess that the finest gifts are spoilt by having to say thank you for them" (Freud and Abraham 1965, pp. 20–21). To say thank you was to be a receiver, a role inimical to one who preferred the role of giver.

As exquisite as his pleasure in giving was Freud's unpleasure in receiving, even in situations where custom dictated that he receive. When Freud arranged with Schur that Schur was to be his physician, he stipulated that he be charged the usual fee rather than be accord professional courtesy. At the end of the year when, at Freud's request, Schur submitted his bill, Freud responded with a letter:

> I am in a quandary as to how to react to the bill you sent me for the past year. If I submitted it to a professional medical organization, you would probably be called upon to account for an unprofessional disregard of medical accomplishment. I feel that you have backed away from the contract upon which our formal relations are based. I do not want to pay this bill and suggest you send me a more appropriate one. [Schur 1972, p. 409]

And probably fearing that Schur might be hurt by the stern formality of the letter as well as to confirm the cordiality of their informal relations, he ended the letter: "With cordial devotion, Your Freud." "The same," Schur writes, "held true with Pichler, whose first notes on Freud contain the following statement: '. . . Patient makes it a condition that he not be treated as a colleague, but be charged [a fee]' " (Schur 1972, p. 409).

Freud regarded his need to provide, even in old age and in illness, a feature of what he called his "father complex." "Leisure is not good for me," he informed Abraham, "because my mental constitution urgently requires me to earn and spend money on my family as the fulfillment of my well-known father complex" (Freud and Abraham 1965, p. 244). The urgency of this need to provide would suggest a need with far deeper roots than that of a father's need to provide: it would suggest, rather, a mother's most primitive need to nurture her offspring. "The only dread I have," he wrote to Eitingon after a long stay at a sanitorium where he was treated for myocarditis, "is of a long invalidism with no possibility of working. . . . I do not possess enough to continue without earning afresh to live as I have, or to fulfill my ceaseless obligations. It is those serious and personal considerations that matter in the last resort" (Jones 1957, p. 121). It was not his suffering as an invalid that mattered in the last resort, but his inability to provide. Similarly to Binswanger when he was seventy-three: "In my failing strength I must still contribute to the support of a number of younger people" (Binswanger 1957, p. 88). When Freud was seventy-three the youngest of his children, Anna, was thirty-nine. When he was seventy-four he divided the greater part of the royalties he received for the eighth edition of *The Interpretation of Dreams* between his sons Martin and Oliver, both in need at that time of financial help. And not surprisingly, there was always concern about his grandchildren.

Freud's so-called father complex embraced not only his family, but also, when he deemed it necessary, the younger of his disciples and, if the situation warranted, a patient in need. In the early days of his association with Freud, Rank had no visible means of support. It was Jones's belief that Freud "partly supported him, without letting anyone else know" (1955, p. 160). Reik too was a beneficiary of Freud's generosity. Sending him to Abraham in Berlin for analysis, he paid for the therapy. "For two years," Reik (1971) writes, ". . . he gave me from his personal pocket a certain amount monthly to study psychoanalysis. I was very poor . . . he gave me money even after I was married for a time" (pp. 87–88). After four years of analysis with Freud, the Wolf Man, relieved of his crippling mental condition, returned to his native Russia, able at last to function. Caught up by the Revolution and stripped of his fortune, he returned penniless to Vienna and again entered treatment with Freud, this time for four months, without paying a fee. And to sustain him and his invalid wife for the next six years, Freud regularly collected sums of money from pupils and colleagues (Jones 1955). Nor did Andreas-Salomé, living in Germany and suffering the privations of the First World War, escape Freud's watchful eye. He arranged with Eitingon, also in Germany, to turn over to her a monthly sum of money. This did not preclude his presenting her with additional sums from time to time, one such time being his own birthday. ". . . this morning," she wrote to Freud, "there arrived from Eitingon, with a kind message in your hand, a most generous present of money. It is as though we had exchanged birthdays, as if it were my birthday" (Freud and Andreas-Salomé 1972, p. 163).

In 1904, Bruno Goetz, an indigent poet-student from Riga studying in Vienna and supporting himself precariously by tutoring and writing occasional newspaper articles, presented himself at Berggasse 19, referred by a professor. Preceding him to Freud's consultation room were several of his poems, sent by the referring professor, presumably as an introduction to the patient. Goetz's ailment was facial neuralgia. Some fifty years later, urged by friends and aided by notes he had made at the time describing his impressions of Freud, Goetz wrote of his visit with "this extraordinary man."

> I looked into his marvelous, kind, warm and melancholy eyes. At the same time it was as if a hand fleetingly touched my forehead—and the pain was as if wiped away. "Oh!" it went through my head, "he is really a medicine man like the Indians have. He doesn't need his whole method. Just as well he might say abracadabra and already one's heart is freer and one feels healthier." That . . . is a physician as he should be! I had never seen such a human being. At once I trusted him completely, unconditionally. [Goetz 1982, p. 285]

Freud encouraged Goetz to talk: " 'Let me get to know you a little . . . tell me something about yourself.' I felt as if a dam had been broken. Before I knew it I had told him about my whole life. . . . What would have been the sense of hiding something from him? Anyhow he knew everything already. . . ." At the end of the interview Freud gave Goetz a prescription for his neuralgia and some advice about diet "and then seemed somewhat embarrassed. 'Don't be offended but I'm a grown-up physician and you are a young student. Please accept this envelope from me and allow me today to play your father, for once. A small honorarium for the pleasure you gave me with your poems and the history of your youth. Goodbye, but come and talk to me again. . . .' " Returning home, Goetz opened the envelope and found two hundred kronen. "I was in such an agitated state that I cried loudly" (Goetz 1982, pp. 285–288). Eissler (1971) estimates that two hundred kronen at that time apparently amounted to Freud's full day's earnings.

Attributing to others his own distaste for receiving, Freud found a way out of this difficulty by making it appear, when possible, that he, the giver, was actually the receiver. Hence, the "small honorarium" he presented to Goetz was a meager return for the pleasure the young student had afforded him with his poems and the history of his youth. In the days of his friendship with Fliess, he sent Frau Fliess, who had been hostess for a short time to him and his brother Alexander on a visit they had made to Berlin, a gift of Venetian glass. Preceding the gift came a letter addressed to her husband: "Tomorrow a little thing made of Venetian glass will be dispatched to our dear hostess; I apologize for it and shall not accept expressions of thanks. It has something about it that, given my uneducated taste and inability to withstand all that Venetian beauty, moved me to possess it, and then I endeavored to double the pleasure through the address to which I sent it" (1985a, p. 137). And to Andreas-Salomé, believing she could not afford the cost of the trip to Vienna she was contemplating at his invitation: ". . . I hope you will allow me to send you from Hamburg the money for the journey. My son-in-law looks after my credit in marks there, and through my earnings in sound foreign currency (American, English, Swiss) I have grown relatively *wealthy*. But I want to have some pleasure out of this new wealth myself" (Freud and Andreas-Salomé 1972, p. 109). As it happened, Andreas-Salomé had the money for the journey, "and I can almost hear it jingling with impatience. Today only many, many thanks and greetings till we meet. . . ." (1972, p. 110). Andreas-Salomé, apparently, did not mind saying thank you. When he received the Goethe prize for literature, Freud instructed his son Ernst to transfer to her 1,000 marks of the money, which had been deposited with him. "In this way," he explained, "I can reduce by a little the injustice which was committed when they awarded the prize to me" (1972, p. 190). The logic of Freud's reasoning seems a bit elusive here. And one wonders what Freud's reaction was to Andreas-Salomé's attitude, so contrary to his own, when she wrote to him on another occasion, ". . . I would never feel ashamed to accept something from you; I only feel the pleasure of gratitude" (1972, p. 119).

Despite his often somber view of life and civilization, Freud was able to feel deeply the everyday pleasures of existence as well. The somber Freud who wrote to his fiancée that he set no great store by life wrote to her sister Minna, in his elation on the eve of his marriage: ". . . the Bodensee is frozen over, and my happy heart is leaping gaily across it" (1985b, p. 131). Freud may not have set great store by life, but he set great store by the good things life had to offer. His disenchantment with civilization did not seem to diminish his enjoyment of those good things. "No, I am not a pessimist," he assured Viereck, "not while I have my children, my wife and my flowers!" (Viereck 1957, p. 11). "I permit no philosophic reflection to spoil my enjoyment of the simple things of life" (Viereck 1957, p. 3). In his paper "On Transience," Freud celebrates the enjoyment of what is enjoyable, its transience making it all the more precious. "Limitation in the possibility of an enjoyment raises the value of the enjoyment. It was incomprehensible . . . that the thought of the transience of beauty should interfere with our joy in it" (1916, 14:305). This sentiment Freud expressed again to Binswanger who, after an operation during which a malignant tumor was discovered and removed, informed Freud of his illness and of the prognosis that he probably had from three to five years to live.[1] ". . . You have only been reminded more forcefully of the uncertainty which keeps all of us in suspense and which one so readily forgets. Now you won't forget it, and life, as you write, will have for you a special and enhanced charm" (Binswanger 1957, p. 39).

Freud's capacity for enjoyment outlived his physical capability to enjoy. One of his greatest pleasures was travel, to see and experience anew. Prevented by illness, he was unable to travel in his old age. In 1935, when he was seventy-nine, he wrote to Arnold Zweig, then living in Palestine: "Your description of spring made me sad and envious. I still have so much capacity for enjoyment that I am dissatisfied with the resignation that is forced on me" (Freud and Zweig 1970, p. 101).

Freud was passionately fond of his family; his children were "my pride and joy." He loved scenic beauty, mountains to climb, pine forests through which he could walk for hours and which served as a hunting ground for mushrooms. If, during a summer's holiday, he could enjoy all three—family, country, travel—he was the most content of men. "The moodiness to which he was subject at other times seemed to disappear altogether in holiday time. Freud certainly displayed then high powers of enjoyment and an extraordinary gusto more often found in those of a younger age" (Jones 1953, pp. 336–337). As naturally as he moved about in the realm of scientific concepts and formulations, he entered the world of his children when he joined them in the country during their

---

[1]Since the tumor was discovered and removed early, actually during an operation for appendicitis, Binswanger survived for many years.

summer holidays, ". . . a full member of our party," Martin writes, "one who shared in our triumphs and disappointments, and I know that he was not playing a part, merely acting to please us. He was truly one of us, naturally and genuinely" (M. Freud 1958 pp. 69–70). He had, says Martin, "*ein froeliches Herz*," not perhaps perfectly translated as "a merry heart" (M. Freud 1958, p. 27). A quality not easily reconciled with the author of *Civilization and Its Discontents*.

Joie de vivre, an attribute of the child as often as of the man of genius, finds its corollary in a characterological naïveté. "It is actually," Eissler reflects, ". . . correlated with the ability that many geniuses possess to regard the world naively . . . as if . . . they were perceiving the world for the first time" (1971, pp. 242–243). This pristine perception would account for the ability of the creative mind to perceive what the sophisticated observer might pass over or ignore. "He [Freud] established," his analysand Joan Riviere writes of him,

> an instantaneous, direct relation to his perception, which automatically excluded cut-and-dried assumptions, or arrière-pensées. Second thoughts and suspended judgment only came much later. The impulse to reject and dismiss at first sight was singularly lacking in him. In using the word naive of him in spite of the usual disparaging connotation, I have done so because it alone, I feel, conveys the strength of this immediate acceptance of whatever he met with as valid. [1956, p. 355]

Hence Freud's immediate and uncritical acceptance of the world of his children, and the recognition in him of a kindred spirit by Jones's five-year-old daughter who, on a visit to Freud with her parents and an older brother, offered him her doll (Jones 1957).

So it was too that Freud, a man without illusions, a "cheerful pessimist," as he called himself, was able to affect those about him with his enjoyment of life, even to the end.

After visiting Freud in London a year before he died, Blanton (1971) wrote: "The overall impression I get of Freud is one of keenness, cheerfulness, alertness, and even gaiety" (p. 102). And Andreas-Salomé, after her visit to Vienna for which Freud had offered to pay the railroad fare: "The most essential result of my stay in Vienna remains the fact that I feel again (what was sometimes difficult enough to feel after one's war experiences) that despite everything life is a marvelous thing" (Freud and Andreas-Salomé 1972, p. 111).

References

Andreas-Salomé, L. (1964). *The Freud Journal of Lou Andreas-Salomé*. New York: Basic Books.

Bernays, A. F. (1940). My brother, Sigmund Freud. In *Freud as We knew Him*, ed. H. M. Ruitenbeek. Detroit: Wayne State University Press, 1973.

Bernfeld, S., and Bernfeld, S. C. (1944). Freud's early childhood. In *Freud as We Knew Him*, ed. H. M. Ruitenbeek. Detroit: Wayne State University Press, 1973.

Bettelheim, B. (1983). *Freud and Man's Soul*. New York: Knopf.

Binswanger, L. (1957). *Freud: Reminiscences of a Friendship*. New York and London: Grune and Stratton.

Blanton, S. (1971). *Diary of My Analysis with Sigmund Freud*. New York: Hawthorn Books.

Bolkosky, S. (1982). The alpha and the omega of psychoanalysis: reflection on Anna O. and Freud's Vienna. *The Psychoanalytic Review* 69: 131–150.

Brandt, L. W. (1966). Process or structure. *Psychoanalytic Review* 53:50–54.

Eissler, K. R. (1971). *Talent and Genius*. New York: Quadrangle Books.

_____ (1985). Biographical sketch. In *Sigmund Freud: His Life in Pictures and Words*, ed. E. Freud, L. Freud, and I. Grubrich-Simitis. New York and London: Norton.

Ellenbogen, H. (1970). *The Discovery of the Unconscious.* New York: Basic Books.

Engelman, E. (1976). A memoir. In *Berggasse 19.* New York: Basic Books.

Feder, S. (1991). Music in mind. In *The American Psychoanalyst.* Vol. 24, No. 4. Hillsdale, NJ: Analytic Press.

Fenichel, O. (1945). *The Psychoanalytic Theory of Neurosis.* New York: Norton.

Freud, A. (1985). In *Sigmund Freud: His Life in Pictures and Words*, ed. E. Freud, L. Freud and I. Grubrich-Simitis. New York and London: Norton.

Freud, H. (1956). My uncle Sigmund. In *Freud as We Knew Him*, ed. H. M. Ruitenbeek. Detroit: Wayne State University Press, 1973.

Freud, M. (1958). *Sigmund Freud: Man and Father.* New York: Vanguard.

Freud, S. (1896). The aetiology of hysteria. *Standard Edition* 3:189–223.

_____ (1899). Screen memories. *Standard Edition* 3:301–322.

_____ (1900). The interpretation of dreams. *Standard Edition* Vols. 4 and 5.

_____ (1901). Psychopathology of everyday life. *Standard Edition* Vol. 6.

_____ (1905). Fragment of an analysis of a case of hysteria. *Standard Edition* 7:3–122.

_____ (1907). Jensen's Gradiva. *Standard Edition* 9:7–95.

_____ (1909). A case of obsessional neurosis. *Standard Edition* 10:153–318.

_____ (1910). Five lectures on psychoanalysis. *Standard Edition* 11:9–55.

_____ (1913). The theme of the three caskets. *Standard Edition* 12:291–301.

_____ (1914). On the history of the psychoanalytic movement. *Standard Edition* 14:3–66.

_____ (1916). On transcience. *Standard Edition* 14:303–307.

_____ (1917). A childhood memory of Goethe. *Standard Edition* 17:146–156.

_____ (1920). Beyond the pleasure principle. *Standard Edition* 18:3–64.

_____ (1921). Group psychology and the analysis of the ego. *Standard Edition* 18:67–143.

_____ (1925). An autobiographical study. *Standard Edition* 20:3–74.

_____ (1926). The question of lay analysis. *Standard Edition* 20:183–258.

_____ (1930). Civilization and its discontents. *Standard Edition* 21:59–145.

_____ (1931a). Female sexuality. *Standard Edition* 21:223–243.

_____ (1931b). Letter to the Burgomaster of Přibor. *Standard Edition* 21:259.

_____ (1933). New introductory lectures. *Standard Edition* 22:3–182.

_____ (1940). An outline of psychoanalysis. *Standard Edition* 23:141–207.

_____ (1954). *The Origins of Psychoanalysis*, ed. M. Bonaparte, A. Freud and E. Kris. New York: Basic Books.

_____ (1960). *Letters of Sigmund Freud*, ed. E. L. Freud. New York: Basic Books.

_____ (1985a). *The Complete Letters of Sigmund Freud to Wilhelm Fliess*, trans. and ed. J. M. Masson. Cambridge, MA and London: The Belknap Press of Harvard University Press.

_____ (1985b). *Sigmund Freud: His Life in Pictures and Words*, eds. E. L. Freud, L. Freud, and I. Grubrich-Simitis. New York and London: Norton.

_____ (1990). *The Letters of Sigmund Freud to Eduard Silberstein*, ed. W. Boelich, trans. A. Pomerans. Cambridge, MA: Harvard University Press.

_____ (1992). *The Diary of Sigmund Freud*, trans. and annotated by M. Molnar. New York: Charles Scribner's Sons.

Freud, S., and Abraham, K. (1965). *The Letters of Sigmund Freud and Karl Abraham*, eds. H. Abraham and E. L. Freud. New York: Basic Books.

Freud, S., and Andreas-Salomé, L. (1972). *Sigmund Freud and Lou Andreas-Salomé: Letters*, ed. E. Pfeiffer. London: Hogarth.

Freud, S., and Breuer, J. (1895). Studies on hysteria. *Standard Edtion., Vol. 2.*

Freud, S., and Jones, E. (1993). *The Complete Correspondence of Sigmund Freud and Ernest Jones*, ed. R. A. Paskauskas. Cambridge, MA and London, England: Harvard University Press.

Freud, S., and Jung, C. G. (1974). *The FreudJung Letters*, ed. W. McGuire. Princeton, NJ: Princeton University Press.

Freud, S., and Pfister, O. (1963). *Psychoanalysis and Faith: The Letters of Sigmund Freud and Oscar Pfister*, eds. H. Meng and E. L. Freud. New York: Basic Books.

Freud, S., and Zweig, A. (1970). *The Letters of Sigmund Freud and Arnold Zweig*, ed. L. Freud. New York: Harcourt, Brace and World.

Gay, P. (1976). Introduction to *Berggasse 19*. New York: Norton.

_____ (1988). *Freud: A Life for Our Time*. New York and London: Norton.

Gedo, J. E. (1992). Art alone endures. *Journal of the American Psychoanalytic Association* 40(2): 501–517.

Goetz, B. (1982). Reminiscences of Sigmund Freud. *The Annual of Psychoanalysis*. Vol. X/1982:281–291. New York: International Universities Press.

Grinstein, A. (1980). *Sigmund Freud's Dreams.* New York: International Universities Press.

H. D. (Hilda Doolittle). (1956). *Tribute to Freud.* New York: Pantheon Books.

Heller, J. B. (1956). Freud's father and mother. In *Freud as We Knew Him*, ed. H. M. Ruitenbeek. Detroit: Wayne State University Press, 1973.

Heller, P. (1992). *Anna Freud's Letters to Eva Rosenfeld.* Madison, CT: International Universities Press.

Holt, R. R. (1992). Freud's parental identification as a source of some contradictions within psychoanalysis. In *Freud and the History of Psychoanalysis*, eds. T. Gelfand and J. Kerr. Hillsdale, NJ and London: Analytic Press.

Jones, E. (1953). *The Life and Work of Sigmund Freud.* Vol. 1. New York: Basic Books.

_____ (1955). *The Life and Work of Sigmund Freud.* Vol. 2. New York: Basic Books.

_____ (1957). *The Life and Work of Sigmund Freud.* Vol. 3. New York: Basic Books.

_____ (1959). *Free Associations.* New York: Basic Books.

Kardiner, A. (1957). The man I knew, the scientist and his influence. In *Freud and the 20th Century*, ed. B. Nelson. Cleveland and New York: World Publishing.

Kris, E. (1954). Introduction. In *The Origins of Psychoanalysis.* New York: Basic Books.

Krüll, M. (1986). *Freud and His Father.* New York: Norton, 1979.

Laforgue, E. (1956). Personal memories of Freud. In *Freud as We Knew Him*, ed. H. M. Ruitenbeek. Detroit: Wayne State University Press, 1973.

Mahony, P. (1982). *Freud as a Writer.* New York: International Universities Press.

_____ (1984). Further reflections on Freud and his writing. *Journal of the American Psychoanalytic Association* 32(4): 847–864.

Molnar, M. (1992). *The Diary of Sigmund Freud.* New York: Charles Scribner's Sons.

Nunberg, H. (1962). *Minutes of the Vienna Psychoanalytic Association*, Vol. 1, ed. H. Nunberg and E. Federn. New York: International Universities Press.

Ornston, D. (1985). Freud's conception is different from Strachey's. *Journal of the American Psychoanalytic Association* 33(2): 379–412.

Pollock, G. H. (1968). The possible significance of childhood object loss in the Josef Breuer-Bertha Pappenheim (Anna O.)-Sigmund Freud relationship. *Journal of the American Psychoanalytic Association* 16:711–739.

Pontalis, J.-B. (1985). Editor's Preface. In *The Freud Scenario*, ed. J.-P. Sartre. Chicago: The University of Chicago Press.

Ransohoff, R. (1976). Captions in *Berggasse 19*, New York: Basic Books.

Reik, T. (1949). *From Thirty Years with Freud*. New York: International Universities Press.

_____ (1953). *The Haunting Melody*. New York: Farrar, Straus and Young.

_____ (1971). *Insights: Conversations with Theodor Reik*, ed. E. Freeman. Englewood Cliffs, NJ: Prentice Hall.

Riviere, J. (1956). A character trait of Freud's. In *Freud as We Knew Him*, ed. H. M. Ruitenbeek. Detroit: Wayne State University Press, 1973

_____ (1991). *The Inner World and Joan Riviere: Collected Papers, 1920–1958*. London and New York: Karnac, 1958.

Roazen, P. (1976). *Freud and His Followers*. New York: Knopf.

Sachs, H. (1944a). *Minutes of the Vienna Psychoanalytic Society*. Vol. 3, New York: International Universities Press, 1974.

_____ (1944b). *Freud: Master and Friend*. Cambridge, MA: Harvard University Press.

Schur, M. (1972). *Freud: Living and Dying*. New York: International Universities Press.

Sterba, R. F. (1982). *Reminiscences of a Viennese Psychoanalyst*. Detroit: Wayne State University Press.

Stewart, W. A. (1967). *Psychoanalysis: The First Ten Years*. New York: Macmillan.

Stolorow, R. D., and Atwood, G. E. (1978). A defensive restitutive function of Freud's theory of psychosexual development. *Psychoanalytic Review* 65:217–238.

Sulloway, F. J. (1979). *Freud, Biologist of the Mind*. New York: Basic Books.

Viereck, G. S. (1957). An interview with Freud. In *Psychoanalysis and the Future*. New York: NPAP.

Wolf, E. S. (1971). *Saxa loquuntur*: artistic aspects of Freud's "The Aetiology of Hysteria." In *Psychoanalytic Study of the Child*. 26:535–554. New Haven, CT: Yale University Press.

Wolf-Man, The (1971). *The Wolf-Man*, ed. H. Gardiner. New York: Basic Books.

Wortis, J. (1954). *Fragment of an Analysis with Freud*. New York: Simon and Schuster.

Credits

The author gratefully acknowledges permission to quote from the following sources:

"Freud and His Mother," by Deborah Margolis, which first appeared in *Modern Psychoanalysis,* the journal of the Center for Modern Psychoanalytic Studies, vol. 14, no. 1, pp. 37–56. Copyright © 1989 by *Modern Psychoanalysis.*

"Freud, Fliess, and the Lost Dream," by Deborah Margolis, which first appeared in *Modern Psychoanalysis,* the journal of the Center for Modern Psychoanalytic Studies, vol. 15, no. 2, pp. 131–148. Copyright © 1990 by *Modern Psychoanalysis.*

Excerpts from "Freud's Mother and Father," by Judith Bernays Heller, in *Commentary,* May 1956, by permission; all rights reserved.

Excerpts from "A Defensive-Restitutive Function of Freud's Theory of Psychosexual Development," by Robert D. Stolorow and George E. Atwood, in *The Psychoanalytic*

Review, vol. 65, no. 2, pp. 218–223. Copyright © 1978 by *The Psychoanalytic Review.*

Excerpts from *Freud: A Life for Our Time,* by Peter Gay. Copyright © 1988 by Peter Gay. Used by permission of W. W. Norton and Company, Inc., J. M. Dent & Sons, Ltd., and the author.

Excerpts from *The Complete Letters of Sigmund Freud to Wilhelm Fliess,* trans. and ed. by Jeffrey Moussaieff Masson, Cambridge, MA: The Belknap Press of Harvard University Press. Copyright © 1985 and under the Bern Convention Sigmund Freud Copyrights Ltd., © 1985 J. M. Masson for translation and editorial matter.

Excerpts from *Freud: Living and Dying,* by M. Schur. Copyright © 1972 by International Universities Press.

Excerpts from *Sigmund Freud and Lou Andreas-Salomé: Letters,* ed. by E. Pfeiffer. Copyright © 1972 by the Hogarth Press. Used by permission of the estate of the author and the Hogarth Press.

From *On the History of the Psycho-Analytic Movement,* translated by Joan Riviere. Copyright © 1962 by James Strachey, renewed © 1991 by Alix Strachey. Copyright © 1966 by W. W. Norton & Company, Inc. Used with their permission and that of Sigmund Freud Copyrights, The Institute of Psycho-Analysis and the Hogarth Press for use of material from *The Standard Edition of the Complete Psychological Works of Sigmund Freud,* trans. and ed. by James Strachey.

From *An Autobiographical Study,* translated by James Strachey. Copyright © 1935 by Sigmund Freud (under the title *Autobiography*), renewed © 1963 by James Strachey. Used by permission of W. W. Norton & Company, Inc. and that of Sigmund Freud Copyrights, The Institute of Psycho-Analysis and the Hogarth Press for use of material from *The Standard Edition of the Complete Psychological Works of Sigmund Freud,* trans. and ed. by James Strachey.

W. W. Norton & Company, Inc. and that of Sigmund Freud Copyrights, The Institute of Psycho-Analysis and The Hogarth Press for use of material from *The Standard Edition of the Complete Psychological Works of Sigmund Freud,* trans. and ed. by James Strachey.

From *Five Lectures on Psycho-Analysis,* translated by James Strachey. Copyright © 1961 by James Strachey. Used by permission of W. W. Norton & Company, Inc. and that of Sigmund Freud Copyrights, The Institute of Psycho-Analysis and The Hogarth Press for use of material from *The Standard Edition of the Complete Psychological Works of Sigmund Freud,* trans. and ed. by James Strachey.

From *Introductory Lectures in Psycho-Analysis,* translated by James Strachey. Copyright © 1920, 1935 by Edward L. Bernays. Copyright © 1965, 1964, 1963 by James Strachey. Used by permission of Liveright Publishing Corporation and that of Sigmund Freud Copyrights, The Institute of Psycho-Analysis and The Hogarth Press for use of material from *The Standard Edition of the Complete Psychological Works of Sigmund Freud,* trans. and ed. by James Strachey.

Selected excerpts throughout from *The Life and Work of Sigmund Freud, Volume 1 1856–1900* by Ernest Jones. Copyright © 1953 by Ernest Jones. Copyright renewed © 1981 by Mervyn Jones. Reprinted by permission of BasicBooks, a division of HarperCollins Publishers, Inc., and Random House UK Limited.

Selected excerpts throughout from *The Life and Work of Sigmund Freud, Volume 2 Years of Maturity 1901–1919* by Ernest Jones. Copyright © 1955 by Ernest Jones. Copyright renewed © 1983 by Mervyn Jones. Reprinted by permission of BasicBooks, a division of HarperCollins Publishers, Inc., and Random House UK Limited.

Selected excerpts throughout from *The Life and Work of Sigmund Freud, Volume 3 The Last Phase 1919–1939* by Ernest

Jones. Copyright © 1957 by Ernest Jones. Copyright renewed © 1985 by Mervyn Jones. Reprinted by permission of BasicBooks, a division of HarperCollins Publishers, Inc., and Random House UK Limited.

Selected excerpts throughout from *Letters of Sigmund Freud,* edited by Ernst M. Freud. Copyright © 1960 by Sigmund Freud Copyrights Ltd. Copyright renewed. Reprinted by permission of BasicBooks, a division of HarperCollins Publishers, Inc., and Sigmund Freud Copyrights.

Selected excerpts throughout from *The Origins of Psychoanalysis: Letters to Wilhelm Fliess* by Sigmund Freud, edited by Marie Bonaparte, Anna Freud, and Ernst Kris. Authorized translation by Eric Mosbacher and James Strachey. Copyright © 1954 by Basic Books Inc. Reprinted by permission of BasicBooks, a division of HarperCollins Publishers, Inc., and Random House UK Limited.

Brief excerpts as submitted from *The Collected Papers, Volumes 1–5,* by Sigmund Freud. Authorized translation under the supervision of Joan Riviere. Published by Basic Books, Inc., by arrangement with the Hogarth Press, Ltd. and the Institute of Psycho-Analysis, London. Reprinted by permission of BasicBooks, a division of HarperCollins Publishers, Inc.

Selected excerpts throughout from *The Interpretation of Dreams* by Sigmund Freud, translated from the German by James Strachey. Published in the United States by Basic Books, Inc., 1956 by arrangement with George Allen and Unwin, Ltd. and the Hogarth Press, Ltd. Reprinted by permission of BasicBooks, a division of HarperCollins Publishers, Inc. and Routledge, UK.

Index